THE CHILD

THE PARENT

AND

THE STATE

DATE DUE

THE CHILD
THE PARENT
AND
THE STATE

James Bryant Conant

HARVARD UNIVERSITY PRESS

Cambridge, Massachusetts

1960

PREFACE

The purpose of this book is to explain some aspects of public education to interested citizens. The four chapters are based on four lectures delivered during the academic year 1958–59. The first and last are revisions of the Pollak and Inglis Lectures given at Harvard University; the second and third have been written from manuscripts of a lecture delivered at Wayne State University and a lecture at Smith College (The Morrow Lecture) respectively. I wish to thank the authorities of the three institutions for permission to use considerable portions of the lectures in the preparation of this book.

Since I had spent the previous academic year in a study of the tax-supported comprehensive high school, the focus of my attention in all four lectures was public secondary education in the United States. Some of the findings of my study and my recommendations for the improvement of public high schools were presented in all the lectures. Rather extensive editorial changes in all but the Inglis Lecture have eliminated, I hope, most of the repetitious portions of the four manuscripts involved and provided some degree of continuity in the exposition. It was both impossible and undesirable, however, to prevent the duplication of certain of the conclusions of my study as presented in *The American High School Today*, published by the McGraw-Hill Book Company in January 1959. (This was "a first report to interested citizens"; the final report will not be forthcoming for some time.) Those who have read my Report will find in portions of Chapter II and Chapter III of this book that I have argued the case for certain of my recommendations in more detail than previously and, I trust, related them to the urgency of the national situation. For the first time, I have considered the difficult and highly controversial subject of financing public education and attempted to sketch briefly some of the issues the thoughtful citizen should have in mind in considering this perplexing subject.

I am greatly indebted to Dr. Reuben H. Gross and Mr. E. Alden Dunham for assistance in the preparation of the original lectures and to Mr. Dunham for much skillful editorial work in the transformation of the lectures into their present form. Miss Betty Jane Watkins' care and patience in the preparation of the manuscript for the printer once again put me in her debt.

JAMES B. CONANT

New York City
June 11, 1959

CONTENTS

THE CHILD
THE PARENT
AND
THE STATE

I

The Child, the Parent, and the State

THE great philosophers from Plato to Whitehead have written about the aims of education; their writings have profoundly influenced the way men and women have thought about the problems of bringing up children; their discussions of the nature of knowledge and the way knowledge is passed on from one generation to another have provided countless teachers with a set of ideas basic to their profession. Yet it is quite evident to anyone who reads books and articles about schools and colleges that when lesser lights have attempted to define education the results more often than not have been neither novel nor illuminating. Over the years I have wrestled with definitions and struggled with chains of logical reasoning; I have been guilty of my share of educational banalities. As a consequence, I must confess to an increasing distrust of the use of the deductive method of thinking about questions confronting teachers.

When someone writes or says that what we need today in the United States is to decide first what we mean by the word "education," a sense of distasteful weariness overtakes me. I feel as though I were starting to see a badly scratched film of a poor movie for the second or third time. In such a mood, I am ready to define education as what goes on in schools and colleges. I am more inclined to examine the present and past practices of teachers than to attempt to deduce pedagogical precepts from a set of premises. Moreover, the empirical approach has many advantages for an educator concerned with explaining the work of teachers to lay audiences. To this I can certify from recent experience. For example, in addressing groups of thousands of citizens in different parts of the country, I found it helpful to an understanding of the problems of our tax-supported schools to stress the differences between certain types of communities as well as the differences between individual children. At all events, in this and the following chapters I shall consider some of the complexities of secondary public education in the United States without attempting to explore the various theories of education.

The starting point for a discussion of our tax-supported schools might well be a consideration of the legal and political structure of our system of education, and this chapter, therefore, will be devoted primarily to the present relation of government to education in this country; or, perhaps I had better say, the relation of government to parents and children. But in order to provide a background for my analysis of current American problems I propose first to range about in both time and space. I shall hope to "frame the target" — to use the old naval ordinance phrase — by examining the relation of organized society to the family in England in the mid-nineteenth century and by noting the relation of youth to the authority of the state in the Soviet Union in 1959. Then I shall try to land a shot very near the center with a few words about German schools as they operate today.

I start by quoting from Matthew Arnold; not from his famous essays, but from his report on continental education published in 1861.[1] Arnold had been sent by the British Government on an inspection tour of schools in France,

Holland, and Switzerland. What he writes about these schools is highly interesting, though what he reveals about the then current attitude of Englishmen towards the state and education is even more illuminating. His words supplement the famous remarks of John Stuart Mill directed against government support of education.[2]

Before 1870, elementary and secondary schools in England were managed and maintained by private organizations. What schools, if any, a child would attend depended solely on the parent. In those days even the famous public schools (in fact private, of course) did not include many from what Arnold calls the "great body of the commercial class," and Arnold goes on to say, "Our middle classes are nearly the worst educated in the world." In contrast stood France with its elaborate system of national education — state supported and centrally controlled — which had solved the problem of "civilizing" the growing power of democracy. The French, so Arnold declares, have "organized democracy with a certain indisputable grandeur and success." In England, on the other hand, "almost everyone believes in the growth of democracy. Almost everyone talks of it, almost everyone laments it; but the last thing people can be brought to do is to make timely preparation for it."

The natural resistance of an aristocracy towards centralized power based in part on memories of the powerful Cromwellian Commonwealth had been reinforced by the fear of the middle-class dissenters that state schools would suffer the same fate as had Oxford and Cambridge after the Restoration — they would become Church of England schools. By the time, however, of the first parliamentary debates on a state system of education in 1870, an important group of dissenters had come around to favoring state schools yet insisted that they should be secular.

3

Mill had argued at length in his essay "On Liberty" against state education but in favor of the state's enforcing universal education by means of public examinations. As an agnostic, he dreaded the possibility that the state would influence "the conclusions of its citizens on disputed subjects"; therefore he insisted that the examinations be confined exclusively "to facts and positive science." His whole treatment of education illustrates the attitude which for a long time prevented the adequate development of free schools in England. To a fear based on the old cleavage of society along religious lines was added a dislike of what some Englishmen had observed in two countries in which free schooling had been rapidly developing — Prussia and the United States.

Apparently, an influential body of opinion had been objecting to proposals for a national education act by pointing to what had happened in these two nations. Arnold admits the validity of these worries and declares boldly "that an English or a French statesman might well hesitate to establish an elaborate system of national education, if it were proved to him that the necessary result of such a system must be to produce effects which have accompanied it elsewhere, to Prussianize his people or to Americanize them." But this is not a necessary consequence, he argues, and quotes his experience in France as evidence to the contrary. How far these arguments affected his fellow citizens, I have no way of knowing. Progress in public education in England was certainly far from rapid in the third quarter of the nineteenth century, and what changes were made seem to me to have been the consequence of industrial competition with both France and a unified Germany after 1870. As an example of the paramount rights of the parent vigorously defended against the state, England in the middle of the last century

4

serves as the right-hand bracket of the target I am defining.

Before jumping to the other extreme, the Soviet Union under the rule of Khrushchev, I venture to intrude a footnote on Arnold's admission of the dangers inherent in Prussian and American education. His words illustrate both how prejudices change and how they linger. Of Prussia, Arnold says: "Under its elaborate system of education, [the Prussian people] has become a studious people, a docile people, a well-informed people if you will — but also a somewhat pedantic, a somewhat sophisticated people. I say that this pedantry, this formalism, takes away something from a people's vital strength. I say that a people loses under them much of the genial natural character, much of the rude primitive vigor, which are the great elementary force of nations." (I may say I have, in my day, heard the Prussians soundly condemned, but never for lack of vigor or elementary force!) As for the Americans, Arnold freely admits they have "not been enervated by education; but under a universal system of comparatively advanced education, without certain correctives, the American people has become an energetic people, a powerful people, a highly-taught people, if you will — but also an overweening, a self-conceited people. . . . This is the capital misfortune of the American people, that it is a people which has had to grow up without ideals. . . . Neither in Church nor in State have [the Americans] had the spectacle of any august institution before their eyes. The face of the land is covered with a swarm of sects, all of them without dignity, some of them without decency. [The Americans] have no aristocracy."

Turning to the awful example of America in another section of the same book, the author raises the question: "On what action may we rely to replace, for some time at any rate, that action of the aristocracy upon the people of this country [England] which we have seen exercise an influence in many respects elevating and beneficial, but which is rapidly and from inevitable causes, ceasing? In other words, and to use a short and significant modern expression which everyone understands [this was written in 1860, remember], — what influence may help us to prevent the English people from becoming, with the growth of democracy, *Americanized?*" Arnold answers this question with what must then have seemed, and still seems, a truly terrifying word. "I confess," he writes, "I am disposed to answer: — *Nothing but the influence of the State.*"

Arnold makes little or no distinction, in his discussion of education and the state, between various ways in which different states are constituted, the forms of government, and the way the government actually supports and directs its schools. This failure makes almost laughable his lumping together centralized France with its revolutionary and Napoleonic traditions, Prussia with its landed aristocracy and military history, and the United States about to be torn apart by a civil war. To my mind, many recent discussions of school systems have suffered from the same failure to push the analysis far enough. In a complex free society deep probing is a tiresome business, as I shall amply demonstrate to the reader by what follows. But in a modern totalitarian state the process is relatively easy. We can all agree that for a considerable period of years the Soviet Union was Stalin. Today, most observers agree that in the Soviet Union the state is Khrushchev. He embodies the state in a way which would make Louis XIV realize how far from reality was his own identification of himself with France.

About the Soviet Union and its schools Americans have been generously supplied with information in the last few years, although, since the Soviet Union is large, reliable

6

school statistics are difficult to obtain and even more difficult to interpret. It is not strange that our picture of the present situation is somewhat blurred. We can, however, be quite clear as to Khrushchev's views and certain that they are already the basis for vigorous reform of the Soviet ten-year schools. Here I wish to present them to serve only as the left-hand boundary of my target, and I shall quote briefly from his memorandum of September 21, 1958.[3] A few extracts will suffice to establish the fact that the interests of the state are considered paramount.

Khrushchev boasts of the expansion of the educational system and attributes the successes in all branches of the national economy to the fact that Soviet schools have been able "to train skilled personnel capable of tackling the most complex and responsible tasks." Yet Khrushchev goes on to say: "There are major shortcomings in the work of our schools and higher educational institutions, and these must no longer be tolerated." The reasons for his profound dissatisfaction touch directly on the problem of the diverse interests of the state and parents. And he leaves no doubt that in the Soviet Union the reconciliation of these interests can be accomplished only in one way — by the firm establishment of the doctrine that the interests of the state are overriding. Here are a few extracts from the memorandum:

"At present our ten-year schools are not accomplishing the task of preparing young people for life but are preparing them solely for admission to higher educational institutions. Among young people who have finished secondary schools, and among families and teaching staffs, there is the firm belief that this is the way it should be, that our secondary schools are designed to train people solely for the purpose of assuring an enrollment for higher educational institutions. ... A number of those who complete ten-year schools reluctantly go to work at factories, plants, and collective and state farms, and some of them consider this to be below their dignity.

"This haughty and contemptuous attitude toward physical work is also to be found in families. If a boy or girl does not study well, the parents and those around the child frighten him by saying that if he does not study well, if he fails to receive a gold or silver medal, he will not be able to get into a higher educational institution and will have to work at a factory as a common laborer. Physical work becomes something with which to scare children."

Khrushchev then goes on to discuss the awarding of medals and the use of competitive entrance examinations for the university and implies that some parents have been exercising influence on the teachers and examiners. And later in the memorandum he writes, "Lastly, we must not ignore the fact that there are still few children of workers and collective farmers in the higher educational institutions. In Moscow's higher schools, for example, children of workers and collective farmers comprise only thirty percent to forty percent of the enrollment. The rest of the students are children of office employees and of the intelligentsia. This situation is clearly abnormal, of course. . . ."

The conclusion of the long indictment of the faults and failures of the Soviet system is that there must be a fundamental reorganization, and Khrushchev gives his opinion that "all students without exception should be drawn into socially useful work at enterprises, collective farms, etc., after completing the seventh or eighth grades. . . . No one should skip this. . . . It is necessary even in the schools to begin preparing people for production, for useful work in society. Give them as much education as possible and then send them into production. Working in production and studying in school, a young person will more easily find his place in society and determine his proclivities and desires. . . . I repeat that there must be no exceptions in this matter, regardless of the parents' status in society or the posts they hold."

This last statement is, for the purposes of this chapter, the significant statement in the memorandum. This is not the place for me to attempt to describe or evaluate the revolution that Khrushchev has decreed in Soviet education.[4] The point is that he has decreed it in the name of the future welfare of the state in terms of producing highly competent technologists and of insuring the stability of a social order based on the premises of Marx and Lenin. And he has ordered it, the objections of any parents to the contrary notwithstanding. All the youth will do as they are told; there will be no exceptions.

The identification of Mr. Khrushchev with the state leaves out the important role of the apparatus of the Communist Party. And the carrying out of Khrushchev's ideas in the Soviet Union is in the first instance a matter for the Central Committee of the Communist Party. For the present, at least, the Central Committee follows his lead. In the Soviet satellite states, the power is not so personalized, if for no other reason than that the supremacy of Moscow must be recognized. In the Soviet Zone of Germany the power structure is somewhat more evident than in the Soviet Union, particularly as regards education and indoctrination. This is so because of the struggle which is still going on to win over the population to the Communist doctrine. Not only do we find the source of educational decisions officially recognized as the Executive Committee of the Socialist Unity Party (the Communist Party in fact), but we can see the Party in action outside the schools. For example, the battle

9

over the minds of the young is openly waged between the churches and the Party. An elaborate initiation ceremony inducting boys and girls into the junior ranks of the Party competes with confirmation. Officially, the state is not involved, though the textbooks and curricula of the schools conform, of course, to the Party line; and university students, whatever their professional field, must study dialectical materialism in order to perfect their knowledge of the doctrines of Marxism-Leninism. It is through the Party, however, that the Communists hope to capture the child and bind him or her to the new order they seek to rivet on the Germans.[5] I imagine the same may be true within the Soviet Union, but since the days of the ideological struggle have passed, we hear much about the schools and little about the out-of-school activities of the Russian youth. Visitors are shown the schools, yet only sophisticated political observers report about the activities of the junior branches of the Communist Party. Information on this important aspect of the behavioral pattern of Soviet youth is, for the most part, lacking.

At this point, some reader is certainly ready to exclaim that neither Khrushchev's views nor those of the English in the nineteenth century have much to do with American schools and colleges. I heartily agree. Having framed the target, let me try to hit somewhere near the center. Let me direct attention to the relation of the child, the parent, and the state in a free nation whose present educational system is far nearer that of the United States than that of Russia now or England a century ago. I refer to the Federal Republic of Germany, whose schools and universities are now little different from what they were in the whole of Germany before the Nazis gained control. Hitler and his gang centralized the educational system, purged it, and made it an instrument for indoctrination. Once they had gained political power and were ready to use it to the full, probably any system of schools would have succumbed in a short time. However, the memories of the Nazis' use of a centralized system of education for their evil ends were undoubtedly one factor which influenced those who drafted the Constitution of the Federal Republic in 1949. For, in place of centralized control, education is today left explicitly to each of the separate states.

Within each state, the management of the schools is centralized in the office of the Minister of Education. The training and appointment of teachers, including their assignment to specific schools, is a matter decided by the Ministry; so, too, are all the details of organization and curriculum. Many matters are determined by the permanent state officials. However, any important changes involve a decision by the Minister, and he, in turn, is guided by the policy of the party in power, for the Minister is a member of the Cabinet of the Minister-President (the equivalent of our governor). The composition of the Cabinet reflects the political complexion of the elected assembly. In spite of a lack of national policy, the pattern of education in all of free Germany appears uniform as compared to the diversity to be found in the United States. This is so because tradition plays a larger role and because the governments of the separate states have made a great effort to establish common practices.[6]

The situation in free Germany, unlike that in the Soviet Union, is one in which parents have a great deal to say about the formal education of their children, though hardly as much as John Stuart Mill thought proper for the England of his day. Until children are about eleven, the choice for most German families is between private and tax-supported education. And all except a small percentage send their children to the tax-supported school. At age eleven the possibility exists of enrolling a child in one of several types of state schools which prepare for the university.[7] These pre-university schools are highly selective in their admission policy and quite ruthless in eliminating pupils who fail to meet the high academic standards of the school during the eight- or nine-year course. The parent whose family tradition indicates a university education for his son, if unsuccessful in enrolling a boy in a tax-supported Gymnasium, will have recourse to a private school and complain about the school authorities and the expense. The numbers of such parents are few, though their influence may be not inconsiderable and could affect, through political channels, the state policy on education.

For one parent who desires to enroll a child in a pre-university school and whose ambition is thwarted, there are probably one hundred who have no such ambition. Family tradition is so vastly more important in Europe than in the United States that Americans often forget that the composition of the pre-university schools so largely reflects the status of the parents. Financial barriers that once blocked the road to higher education have been largely removed, and in some districts in some cities I have no doubt that conscientious teachers endeavor to urge all bright children to apply for admission to one or the other type of pre-university school. But many, many parents have no interest in having their offspring proceed along such an unusual road — that is, unusual for the family in question. No one can begin to estimate how much academic talent fails to be developed by suitable education because of the attitude of some types of parents of bright children. There is little the state can do about it. And at present, with the universities overcrowded, only a few Germans are concerned about this aspect of their system.[8]

At long last I come to the United States. Anyone at all familiar with the American schools will already have noted the similarities between some of our problems and those I have been discussing. Not many years ago, a considerable body of opinion in this country would have had great sympathy with those Englishmen who in the 1850's and 1860's thought that what happened to children was a matter for the parents to decide. The state should not come between a father and his son. I used to hear such arguments when I was young from those opposed to the movement to abolish child labor by federal and state laws. These arguments would sound archaic today. The health of young people is now admittedly the concern of both the state and the federal government. Federal funds provide school lunches; in every state a mass of laws regulates the employment of the young, their consuming habits, and their modes of locomotion. The freedom of the parent is considerably circumscribed as compared with even sixty years ago. He may want his child to take a certain job, but the state laws may prohibit the employer from acceding to the parent's wishes. Even if the parent owns a car and believes his boy capable of driving it alone, the state laws governing the issuance of a license determine the legality of the boy's driving.

In regard to schooling, a parent in every state in the United States has one choice at least — namely, the choice of sending his offspring to a private school or to a tax-supported school. This choice was insured by a decision of the Supreme Court of the United States in 1925.[9] In all except three states, children must attend some school recognized as satisfactory by the state authorities until reaching the age of sixteen or seventeen. Indeed, in five states, full-time education is compulsory until eighteen or until high school graduation.[10] One must note, as a modification of the full-time education requirements, certain provisions for those who, having reached a certain age, can obtain a job and want to leave school prior to high school graduation. The regulations governing such matters are so complex and vary so much from state to state as to make impossible any attempt at brief description.[11] Those who are interested will find further discussion of this subject in the concluding pages of this book.

Before considering the way in which the state may regulate the kind of school to which the parent may send his child, let me examine the standard arguments for compulsory education as a limitation on parental rights. From these arguments flows the necessity of providing adequate free schooling, for, clearly, it would be almost inconceivable that the sovereign authority of a state would demand full-time education and then not be prepared to provide this education without expense to all the citizens. Whether or not those phases of education which are not prescriptive should be supported by the taxpayer is quite another subject.

The argument one used to hear from those who wanted more and better public schools was that a representative form of government could survive only if the electorate was well educated. To the recalcitrant taxpayer, the belligerent educator used to say, in effect: "Shell out, or someday an angry, illiterate mob will take your riches from you." (Some will remember Macauley's famous prophecy about the inevitable downfall of democracy and President Garfield's answer to the effect that the British historian had left out of account universal education.) In addition to the argument for free schooling for all American youth based on the need for education for citizenship, one heard another that goes back to Jefferson to the effect that in a democracy careers must be freely open to the talented.[12] The taxpayer must support free schools (even if his children do not attend them) because schools, as ladders of opportunity, are an essential element in our democracy, a society which must be prevented from hardening along caste lines.

Compulsory attendance for a considerable period of years in an approved school is one limitation which the state today places on the freedom of the parent. A second concerns the educational offerings in the tax-supported schools. As everyone familiar with American education knows, the courses offered in a high school are determined to a large degree by the local school board or its equivalent. Likewise, the way instruction is presented in the elementary schools will vary from community to community depending on decisions of the school boards and their appointed officials. Of course, the local school board can be thought of as representing the power of the state, for all its authority has been delegated to it by actions of the state legislature or by the state constitution. Nevertheless, it is convenient to examine separately the powers exercised by the local authority as contrasted with state-wide regulations.[13] This difference, which some may regard as purely theoretical, has great practical significance. As compared to any other country in the world, collectively American parents have enormous influence on their schools. This is true in most communities and is a consequence of our system of local control through elected school boards whose members are bound to listen to the pleas of outraged fathers and mothers. The school boards are by no means indifferent to what parents may say, nor are the officials appointed by the school boards.

The situation in the large cities is unusual, for in the large city the school board is almost as far removed from the parents as is the state legislature. Elsewhere, one may say that the state, in the form of its agent, the local board, is in close touch with the parents and vice versa.

The contrast with Europe is worth noting. In the United States, many decisions which in Germany, for example, would be made by the Ministry of Education are made by the local board. Important educational matters are settled by a school board responding in part to the views of parents, in part to the pressure exerted by taxpayers who are not parents, in part to representations made by the teachers, and often to the advice of the superintendent and his staff. Under these conditions it is clear that if there were no traditional pattern in American education, there would be literally thousands of very different schools. Actually, there is a traditional pattern and far more uniformity than might be imagined, because educators are basically conservative in spite of what laymen think! The differences from school to school, however, are highly significant and often represent the differences between a satisfactory and an unsatisfactory school, particularly from the point of view of providing adequately for a wide spectrum of abilities. Such differences are an inevitable consequence of the high degree of independence of the local school board and, to an extent, reflect the diversity of the parental interest between one type of community and another.

In retrospect, it is easy to see that a responsiveness of the management of a school system to the desires of parents has resulted, in more than one community, in schools that have failed to challenge sufficiently the potentially able student. But in the relatively relaxed days of the past, even in the Depression and certainly in the boom days of the

1920's, few argued about education in terms of specific needs of society. The emphasis was on education for citizenship and on developing an understanding of democracy among the entire youthful population of the country. It was assumed that in a flexible society there would be enough doctors educated every year to handle our problems, enough engineers and scientists to take care of national needs. (I even remember when a Ph.D. in chemistry had difficulty in locating a job, and this was long before the Depression.) People were remarkably indifferent as to whether parents chose to take advantage of the educational opportunities offered, and local authorities sometimes were not very strict in enforcing the compulsory attendance laws. In other words, as long as the public concern was directed almost exclusively to the education of future voters and the unfolding of the personality of each child, a thousand very different schools might be considered an excellent idea. Few could claim to have the one and only prescription for the kind of education that would produce the results desired.

World War II provided the first shock to citizens and to educators who started from the premise of the independence of each child, if not of each parent. What was accomplished or not accomplished in school or college obviously did have a great deal to do with winning the war in the shortest time and with the minimum expenditure of lives. There was, for the time being at least, an overriding state interest, the state being now the national government, which could draft male youth whether or not parents liked it. And World War II, unlike World War I, called for more than courageous youth with a general education. There was a demand for technical specialists of all sorts. Most of the specialists needed mathematical training. The number of able males with particular aptitudes and skills suddenly became a matter of national interest. After the war, this interest never died. On the contrary, it was heightened, as more and more Americans came to realize we were in a cold war in a highly technical age. The spotlight was thrown on phases of the work of our free schools which had hitherto excited little interest. People began to bewail the fact that many bright boys and girls stopped their education at the end of high school or before. Individually, the decision made might be good or bad, but more and more the question was raised: Can we afford to let our talent go untrained?

As a consequence of this new mood, we find ourselves in a rather mixed-up state of mind about the relation of the child, the parent, and the state. Recognizing the traditional extent to which the local school board exercises the authority of the state, some people are demanding more centralized state control of all the public schools. Indeed, there are those who talk about the federal government setting standards, though just what is meant by "the federal government" is far from clear.

In considering proposals for more centralized control of our public schools, the first question to answer is: To what degree is it possible or desirable to have a uniform school curriculum throughout a given state? We are here concerned with the division of authority between the state authorities and the local school boards. There are many arguments in favor of leaving a high degree of initiative to the local boards. If this were not done, one would have something approaching a European system of schools, even if the hiring of teachers still remained a local matter. Freedom to experiment with different procedures all through the elementary and secondary schools has been a cherished principle of American educators and of parents as well. That this experimentation should be kept within a certain framework almost all would certainly agree, but, as I pointed out earlier, this framework is very largely supplied by the traditions of the profession. In addition to the advantages that flow from local initiative, it is easy to establish that communities within a given state vary in some respects in regard to their educational needs. In Chapter III, I shall take the reader on an imaginary trip to schools in two very diverse communities.

Another factor which limits the possibility of establishing a uniform state pattern is the diversity of the student body in the high school years. In the European states, on the other hand, those schools which are attended by the majority provide full-time education only through age thirteen. It is relatively easy under such conditions to establish a state-wide curriculum because, as in our first eight grades, all students must be taught the same basic skills. In the selective pre-university schools, the state is dealing with a relatively homogeneous student body with specific academic objectives, and a state curriculum can be planned and justified.

When the great transformation of American public education occurred between 1905 and 1930 (a subject I shall treat in detail in the concluding chapter), a new situation was created for those who were concerned with the high school curriculum. It was in this period that the high school became widely comprehensive, and teachers and administrators were faced with the task of providing adequate education for *all* American youth. Leaving aside the desire for experimentation and the stimulation of local initiative, a prescribed course of study in grades one through twelve for *all* pupils within a state is not possible, as I shall demonstrate in detail in a later chapter. The real question is: What limits can and should the state place on the curricular offerings in the local schools? Let us see what has actually happened in recent times.

There is a great variety among the states in regard to how much is prescribed from the state capital to the local boards.[14] There are states where there is practically no state requirement as to the subjects which must be offered or satisfactorily completed in order to obtain a high school diploma. There are other states in which rather detailed prescriptions are laid down in both regards. About three quarters of the states have requirements for graduation from high school involving five or more units in particular subject areas. Perhaps it would be useful to give a few illustrations from this rather confusing national scene.

The Board of Regents of the State of New York (the state board of education) sets forth a minimum program of courses which must be completed by a student in order to graduate from a public high school. These courses include four years of English, three years of social studies including one year of American history, one year of science, one year of mathematics (a new requirement in 1961 for a Regents' diploma), one-half year of health education or its equivalent, and a three-year elective sequence in one of a number of fields. In addition, physical education without credit is required for at least two school periods a week each semester.

The graduation requirements, it should be noted, are mandated by the Regents. In addition to the Regents' regulations, there are requirements enacted by the New York State legislature. For example, each year between the third and tenth grades all students must receive instruction regarding the nature and effects of alcohol for not less than three lessons a week for ten or more weeks or the equivalent.[15] (I might note parenthetically I have not seen evidence that such instruction has reduced the consumption of alcoholic beverages!) For all students over eight years of age there must be instruction in patriotism and citizenship and, for all students above the eighth grade, instruction in the United States Constitution, the Declaration of Independence, and the State Constitution. Fire prevention, highway safety, the meaning of various holidays, the nature and effects of narcotics, the humane treatment of wildlife, the use of firearms — these are still other subjects touched upon by legislative enactment. In almost all states, the legislatures have enacted statutes covering some of these and other matters which are to be included in the curriculum of the schools.

New York is an example of a state with a rather detailed curriculum prescription, uniform throughout. Two other examples of nearby states may help illustrate the diversity that we find in the United States. The State Board of Education in New Hampshire just recently moved in the direction of New York by announcing certain minimum standards to be required of all students for graduation and certain minimum standards that all high schools should meet in regard to course offerings. Apparently there was resistance to this action, and the Attorney General of New Hampshire has ruled that under existing statutes the State Board does not have the authority to impose such standards on the public schools.[16] Here is an open clash between parental rights as expressed locally and centrally mandated statewide standards. To move to an opposite extreme from New York, we find in Connecticut that the only statute or administrative requirement for graduation from a public or private high school is a course in American history. The contrast with New York needs no underlining.

New York is by no means alone in prescribing many details of the educational offerings in the local public high schools and the requirements for a diploma. It is unique, however, in having statewide syllabi, examinations, and diplomas. The importance of the syllabi lies in the fact that Regents' examinations, used throughout the state for nearly one hundred years, are based upon them. The examinations themselves are not mandated for all pupils, nor do they exist in all courses, but should a school choose not to use Regents' examinations, its program must be approved by the state. There is by no means unanimous agreement as to the effect of these examinations. Some professionals see them as a means of achieving quality education in the state, whereas others see them as a deterrent to local initiative and experimentation, since teachers may be tempted to follow the Regents' syllabi too closely, to teach for the examinations only. Related to the examinations is the Regents' diploma, which may be issued if a student completes a course of study including at least eighteen units in grades nine through twelve (effective 1961) and passes Regents' examinations in certain designated subjects. The diploma is not limited to students pursuing strictly academic work, and the examinations themselves cover a wide variety of courses. However, to promote scholarship in view of the new mood of the American public, the Regents recently initiated special scientific and honors diplomas. Actually, the issuance of Regents' diplomas is not mandatory, and I know of at least one school which uses the examinations as a kind of check on itself without encouraging its students to apply for a Regents' diploma.

New York is unique, also, in having in the Board of Regents perhaps the oldest and most powerful state board of education in the country. In existence since 1784, the Board of Regents is composed of citizens serving for a period of thirteen years, one from each of the ten judicial districts and three appointed at large. A member is elected by the joint action of the two houses of the legislature in the State of New York. The State Constitution makes the Regents head of the State Education Department and gives them power to appoint and remove the Commissioner of Education. Over the years, the Board of Regents has developed such traditions that membership on the board, which is without compensation, carries great prestige. It is clear that a board with this long history and with its members holding office for so many years is bound to be a very powerful influence on education in a state. Both the Board of Regents and its appointee, the Commissioner of Education, are independent of the Governor. In no other state has a state board of education the same continuity and the same degree of power; likewise, the power of the Commissioner is vast indeed as compared to that of the chief school officer in other states. In some states, this officer (the equivalent of the Commissioner of Education in New York) is elected; in many others, he is appointed by the governor. Various schemes have been tried for appointing the state board of education. In short, there is no uniformity in this field. There are many students of the subject who feel that the chief school officer should be independent of the governor and should be an appointee of the state board of education, whose members should hold office for a relatively long period of years.[17]

It is worth calling the reader's attention to the fact that even the New York system is highly decentralized as compared to that of a German state, where the recruiting, training, and placing of teachers is a function of the state Ministry of Education. Teachers are assigned to local schools as the central authority sees fit. Under such conditions, something approaching uniformity in the quality of the teaching can be assured; under such conditions and with state exam-

inations playing an important role in the educational process, the schools throughout a given state have comparable
standards. It is possible to talk about what one likes and
dislikes in such a system of state schools. Even in New York
State, however, one is dealing with a system of schools
essentially locally controlled, and it is difficult to make meaningful statements about such a system except by examining
the situation city by city and town by town. To be sure,
the minimum requirements for a diploma are uniform
throughout the state, but important as New York's minimum standards are, their existence does not answer a number of highly significant questions. During my visits to
schools throughout the country, I found satisfactory schools
in a state with practically no minimum requirements at all,
and I found unsatisfactory schools in states with many requirements. Unless one were prepared to accept the continental tradition and establish a system of state schools, I
believe no set of state regulations can insure schools of uniform excellence, and I for one would certainly not be prepared to argue for any such radical change in the basic
American pattern.

At first sight, those who are worried about the shortcomings of our public schools might be inclined to urge all
other states to copy New York. But I am not sure that I
would agree. There are three dangers to be noted if one
proceeds *rapidly* to increase the power of the state exercised
at the state level. First, the legislature itself may decide to
take a hand at regulating details of school curricula through
statutory enactment. This has already happened in regard to
American history, the history of certain states, and physical education. Legislative bodies are not well adapted to
making wise educational decisions — snap votes and riders
on appropriation bills are usually far from well considered.
Second, a regulatory agency like a central state board may

be made up of the wrong people. A state school board needs time to build a tradition of the sort one finds in New York. Such a centralized body, ready to exercise vast power, unguided by a tradition, may easily turn out to be a board composed largely of self-seeking politicians. So, too, is more than one local board, of course, though the errors made at the local level affect only one city or town and are more easily reversed than those made at the state level. Third, attempts may be made to introduce quite unrealistic proposals which will do more harm than good; fanatics will ride a hobby hard, and an unseasoned board without traditions and without the leadership of a first-rate chief state school officer may adopt some wild ideas. A few years ago the danger might have been that certain types of social studies courses would have been forced on all the schools. At the moment, the danger lies in the other direction — that exposure to advanced mathematics and science will be required of *all* the students in high school. (I use the word "exposure" advisedly.) A proposal was made in 1958 in the Georgia legislature that all high school students be required to study four years of science and four years of mathematics — an absurd idea.[18] It may be well for some states to move in the direction of the *slow* development of a system like that of New York State, but hasty steps in this direction are certainly not to be recommended.

Thus far, I have been considering the relation of public authority as exercised at the state or local level to such matters as the content of the school curriculum and the requirements for a high school diploma. Obviously, there are many other aspects of primary and secondary education which are the responsibility of some governmental agency, be it the state board of education, the commissioner of education, or the local school board. One is the training and certification of teachers, another is financing the schools.

Historically, state concern with the quality of the teaching is one of the earliest examples of the state, as such, being involved with the local schools. The Board of Education of Massachusetts established the first state normal school for the training of teachers in Lexington, Massachusetts, in 1839.[19] Since then it has been widely assumed that each state has a duty to provide essentially free instruction beyond the high school for those who wish to become teachers. In all states today, state teachers' colleges, state universities, or their equivalent, exist and are controlled from the state capital in one way or another and financed largely, if not entirely, by state funds. Along with provisions for the relatively free education of public school teachers has gone the establishment by the state of minimum educational requirements for those who wish to enter the professional field of education. As in the case of the control of the content of the curriculum, there is enormous variety between the states — ranging from Massachusetts, where teachers need twelve semester hours of professional educational courses for a certificate, to Washington, where twenty-seven hours are required.[20] In many states, it is possible to obtain a temporary certificate without meeting the formal requirements, but in order to obtain a permanent position the candidate must present evidence of having completed work in the fields of both the liberal arts and education. The fact that a graduate of a liberal arts college who has specialized in a given field such as chemistry, English, or history cannot obtain a permanent certificate in many states has led to much bitter feeling on the part of many professors of the liberal arts. However, I postpone a consideration of the quarrels among educators until the third chapter. I must find space to outline, at least, the highly complicated, but vital, subject of school finances.

Four generalizations are possible about the financing of

our public schools. First, in every state the funds for the support of the local system come in part from local real estate taxes and in part from taxes levied by the state itself. Second, in no state is the amount of money now available adequate in every community in the state. Third, to find a satisfactory formula according to which state funds may flow to school districts on an equitable basis to supplement the local financial provisions has taxed the skill and ingenuity of lawyers, legislators, and economists to the very limit. Fourth, the need for a formula comes from the fact that the real estate base for local taxes has, by and large, proved totally inadequate. There probably is no one completely satisfactory scheme. For the state to take over entirely the financing of each school district would be, of course, to move far in the direction of a system of state schools. Unless a local community, through its school board, has some control over the purse, there can be little real feeling in the community that the schools are in fact local schools. I have heard the opinion expressed by those who have devoted much study to the matter that something like 50 percent of the current expenditures should be raised through local taxes if local control is to predominate. Taking the country as a whole, the percentage of total revenue appropriated for public schools from state funds rose from 15.8 in 1930 to 39.0 percent in 1950, and in 1955–56 was 39.5 percent.[21] The 1957–58 figure was 40.8 percent. A survey of the situation state by state shows the enormous diversity in practice. In Delaware, the fraction of state aid in 1957–58 was 88.2 percent; in a few other states, the figure was about 70 percent; and in Nebraska, only 6.9 percent of the school expenses were provided by state taxes.[22]

At the risk of vastly oversimplifying a tangled and complex matter, one may say that today in most states in which state aid plays an important role two somewhat different ideas are involved in the justification of the policy. One can be thought of as a per capita grant of state-collected money, the other a foundation or equalization program. As to the first, a state tax — be it a state income tax, a state excise tax, or a state property tax — can be thought of as a collection of revenue from the whole state for the benefit of all the people in the state. From this thought follows the notion that some of this money might well flow to the local communities on a per capita basis. If earmarked for education, this type of state aid might be considered a form of tax sharing. In the larger states in which I have visited schools, the consequence of this policy was that even some school districts with very large local resources received some state money which one could not help thinking might have been better spent in school districts not far away that had very meager local resources. Taken by itself, the flat per capita "grant" (whether on the basis of the total population in the district or per child in attendance in a public school) has been felt by many educators to be inadequate.

The idea of a foundation program was promulgated some years ago. The state, it was argued, had not only a duty to set minimum standards for all schools within the state, but a duty to provide state money in such amounts that the state and local revenues would provide together a minimum financial base for all school districts. Once this was provided, so it was argued, there would be room for local initiative to raise even more local taxes and provide a school considerably above the minimum. In many communities, this could not happen if the tax resources locally were strained to the limit in providing the local share under a flat grant program.

Basic to the concept of a foundation program is the realization of the fact that school districts even within the richer states vary enormously in the value of the real estate on which local taxes must be raised. As one visits schools and asks about the financial basis for their support, one is deeply impressed by the inequities in the situation. A large manufacturing plant may be located in one district which, therefore, has a high real estate valuation and, with a very low tax rate, can raise funds for an adequate school system. Most of the employees in this plant, however, may live in another city or town in which the real estate valuation is low, and the school district which is really serving the plant is quite unable, out of local tax receipts, to provide even a minimum program. However, the further a state goes towards defining exactly the foundation program, determining what is the amount of tax that a district *ought* to raise and then supplying the rest, the further it moves towards a system of state schools. Furthermore, an equalization program that would send state money only to some districts and provide no benefits at all to others is not likely to recommend itself to an assembly of representatives of all parts of a given state.

I have attempted to outline two basic considerations that enter into any discussion of the state and local financing of public schools. Another that should be mentioned is the question of valuation of real estate. For the operation of an equitable equalization program, a uniform method of assessing real estate throughout the state is almost essential. Yet in many states the machinery for making the assessment is far from insuring uniformity. Still another complication must be noted. State laws and sometimes provisions of the state constitution put limits on the taxing power of the local school board. There are various devices by which the legislatures in different states have attempted to protect the owner of real estate from unjustified demands for higher taxes to support the schools. I shall make no attempt even to indicate the variety of such provisions.

In addition to state and local funds, many schools receive

also some money from the federal government, not directly, but through a centralized state agency. Leaving aside the provisions for school lunches and a few special cases such as federally impacted areas, it is safe to say that until very recently the bulk of the money came from congressional appropriation for vocational education. The authorization for these annual grants started with the Smith-Hughes Act of 1917 and has been broadened by subsequent legislation.[23] If we leave the field of secondary education and consider higher education, we must turn back to the famous Morrill Act passed during the Civil War. The so-called land-grant colleges which were set up in each state to obtain federal funds under this authorization now include some of the largest and most flourishing of our state universities. Though the fraction of their revenue which comes from the federal government is small, the money still continues to arrive from Washington. Since World War II, this federal contribution to higher education has been overshadowed by the enormous sums which are provided by congressional appropriation for research and development and are spent in colleges and universities throughout the land. One can almost speak of the revolutionary transformation of American higher education as a consequence of the flood of federal money which now inundates the institutions of higher learning in the form of grants or under contracted arrangements. But this subject lies outside the scope of the present volume.

The National Defense Education Act of 1958 set a somewhat new pattern.[24] Congress is authorized to appropriate considerable sums of money to the separate states for specific purposes. Both secondary and higher education are involved, yet no appreciable help will come, as a consequence of this Act, to the school districts whose costs per pupil are below any reasonable standard. Not that the Act may not prove beneficial in the long range to public secondary education. It certainly will be beneficial by providing facilities for improving the training of guidance officers and foreign language teachers, for example, just as the federal money allocated by the National Science Foundation for summer courses for mathematics and science teachers has been most beneficial in improving the quality of the instruction in these subjects.[25]

To those educators who realize the extent of the handicap under which many, many school districts are working, none of the existing federal statutes is at all adequate. What these people demand, and have for a generation advocated, is a continuing annual congressional appropriation of a very large amount to go to each state to supplement the state funds which are used to support the local schools. Days of testimony on this subject, pro and con, have been taken by congressional committees over the last twenty years. A bill drawn up and sponsored by Senator Taft actually passed one branch of Congress some years ago, but, to date, Congress has been unwilling to engage in a new type of educational support. Whether, in view of the present mood of the American people, the time has come for the opening of a new chapter in American public education through massive federal aid is, for me, a perplexing problem. Before discussing the pros and cons of federal aid for the general purposes of public schools, I shall ask the reader to consider the exigencies of the present situation. The next chapter opens with a discussion of the impact of our struggle with Soviet imperialism on educational planning. After a consideration of some of the reforms demanded by the dangers of the international situation, I shall review briefly the question of where we are to obtain the funds to do the job which must be done if our tax-supported schools are to play their proper role in the preservation of our freedom.

II

Education in the Second Decade
of A Divided World

As the title of this chapter indicates, I do not believe we can divorce a discussion of our schools from a consideration of the kind of world in which we live. And let us be frank about it — it is not an entirely pleasant world. Quite the contrary. Those whose memory goes back to the days before the first World War will probably agree that when we were young the present international situation would have been for us literally inconceivable. Even those who remember only the early 1930's would probably assent to the proposition that in their youth few, if any, would have credited a prophecy of a future in which two powers faced each other armed with new weapons, a single one of which could destroy a large-sized city. Yet that is the kind of world in which we live, and I see no prospects of an amelioration of the situation, at least for many years to come.

This picture, which would have seemed too terrible to be believed by my generation thirty or forty years ago, did not develop overnight. We have had time to accustom ourselves somewhat to the horrors. The atomic bomb became a reality in the closing days of World War II. The fusion bomb and the possibility of its delivery by an intercontinental rocket came later — after we had a chance to become used to learned professors debating the probability of the continued existence of civilization. I wonder how many readers recall the best-selling pamphlet of the immediate post-war years — "One World or None"? And how many recall Elmer Davis' reply to the authors — "If necessary, none"? By which he meant if it came to a choice between capitulation to the Soviets or an atomic war, he, for one, chose the latter.

In the late 1940's we learned to live with the failure of our first hopes about atomic energy. No agreement could be reached with the Soviets as to the control of the manufacture of atomic bombs. And just as the fearful prospects of a gigantic armament race loomed over the horizon, all doubts were resolved about the Soviets' intentions in Europe. The coup d'état in Prague and the Berlin Blockade opened the eyes of almost all who still clung to the belief that cooperation with our erstwhile ally was still possible. Furthermore, a new and menacing phrase was added to our vocabulary — "Red China." Yet hopes for what some called a "People's Peace" died hard. I recall that when in 1948 I ventured to predict that the world would remain deeply divided for many years to come, I was considered far too pessimistic. Of course, there were others who felt that my second forecast of a period of high tension without a global war was far too sanguine. It happens that both prophecies have so far been correct. This is no warrant, of course, for their validity for an indefinite future. But I shall take them nonetheless as premises for my present discussion of American education.

In most respects, the international situation is the same now as it was when I wrote *Education in a Divided World* ten years ago.[1] To my mind, the replacement of atomic bombs carried in airplanes by fusion bombs attached to rockets does not introduce a really novel factor. It was clear that the destructive power of the new weapons was going to increase with the passing years and that both sides in the armament race would have to devote increasing amounts of manpower and money to the development of offensive and defensive weapon systems. What is new, it seems to me, are the political developments in areas of the world which in the late 1940's seemed not to be the focus of our troubles. I refer, of course, to the growing nationalism in many underdeveloped portions of the world and the successful infiltration of Soviet influence in vast areas heavily populated with impoverished people. The struggle for the uncommitted countries, on the one hand, and the increasing ferment in the Middle East and Africa, on the other, have time and again in the last few years presented the governments of the free nations with a choice between only thoroughly bad alternatives.

During the first decade of the divided world, it was obvious that the United States was for the first time in its history a world power with vast responsibilities for leadership. Opposed stood a second world power bent on global domination and whose strength was growing. It was clear that we had to be strong — economically, politically, and militarily — and, at the same time, build solidarity among the free peoples. The Marshall Plan was a blueprint for such building. Now in the second decade we realize we must do still more. We must help the peoples in the uncommitted nations to resist the encroachment of the Communist doctrines. For if the Soviets should be able to repeat in other parts of the globe their success in China, we in the free world would be very near disaster. Can anyone look at the map and the population figures and question this conclusion?

Do we Americans in our thoughts and acts respond to the stark realities of the situation? I doubt it. As I have traveled around the United States during the last two years, visiting schools and talking with educators and many other people, I sense no feeling of urgency in most places. People are for the most part remarkably carefree and complacent. Yet few would challenge the correctness of the broad outlines of the grim picture I have sketched. Even during the recurrent periods of high international tension, few seemed to worry about what would happen. That there has been no panic when the international outlook blackened is, in one sense, excellent; collectively, we have proven to have steady nerves in the darkest hours of an atomic age even in the face of threatened military action. Not many would have predicted such behavior when the atomic bombs first entered our calculations. But there is the other side of the coin. Are we worried enough about those matters which deserve attention if we are to survive the ordeals ahead — if we are to continue strong, keep our allies among free nations, and prevent the present neutrals from drifting into the other camp? My answer would be "no"; we are not worried enough about the future and about areas of action where we could do more to insure our meeting the Soviet competition. And, of these areas, I have in mind particularly education.

In describing the present scene and indicating what requires action, we must be cautious about generalizations. Our colleges and universities are so numerous and so diverse that I fail to see how anyone can generalize about them. I am sure a foreign observer would wonder why there was not more agreement among the nearly two thousand institutions as to ways in which effective cooperation could be attained. And he would be surprised to see how much competition among colleges and universities now exists even in the face of the wave of increased numbers. He might be surprised that so few states seem to have planned effectively for cooperation between the various tax-supported two-year and four-year institutions.[2] But foreigners never can understand our higher educational chaos. They likewise fail to understand our pattern of public education, with the responsibility for our schools largely in the hands of thousands and thousands of local school boards. And I have gradually come to the conclusion that many Americans do not understand the pattern either, and some at least will not take the trouble to understand it. For example, it has been amazing to me since the Russian success with rockets how many thoroughly ill-informed persons have taken it upon themselves to criticize *the* American high school. They speak as though it were possible to characterize the typical American high school, or to cite meaningful national statistics about the number of youth studying trigonometry, or the percentage of high schools offering a course in physics.[3]

There are 21,000 American public senior high schools. (I mean schools which graduate a senior class.) I would not know how to go about trying to answer the question: Are these schools doing a good job? I can only say that I know of some that are and many that are not. But it would take a truly mammoth study to get an answer about all 21,000 that would have any chance of being valid. One bit of reliable information about these schools, however, is available. And I think it points to a serious national problem that nine citizens out of ten ignore when they criticize our tax-supported schools. I refer to the size of the high school and the percentage of the youth of high school age in each state attending high schools of insufficient size.

I am prepared to demonstrate that high schools with a graduating class of much less than one hundred cannot do justice to those enrolled except at exorbitant expense. This fact follows from the comprehensive non-selective nature of the American high school, about which I shall have more to say in subsequent chapters. A good high school in an average American community should offer a variety of elective programs occupying about half the students' time; these should include a variety of courses designed to develop skills marketable on graduation (carpentry or auto mechanics for boys, stenography for girls, for example). For the academically talented, there should be courses in physics, chemistry, twelfth-grade mathematics, and one or more foreign languages. But in a small high school there are so few who would enroll in the different programs that providing the equipment and adequate instructors is prohibitively expensive. As a consequence, in these schools few elective courses are usually available, a watered-down academic program is the fare provided for all pupils. Such a situation is bad for the entire student body, but let me first concentrate attention on the nation's loss because of the neglect in the small high schools of those boys and girls (particularly the boys) who have the capacity to study advanced mathematics, science, and a foreign language.

In some states, as many as two thirds of the youth of high school age are attending schools with a graduating class of less than one hundred. The country over, something like a third of our youth are attending high schools that are too small. As a result, one of the most precious assets of the nation is being squandered — the potential talent of the next generation. It is almost impossible for students graduating from many of the small schools later to become members of the learned professions. Medicine, engineering, and science are careers practically barred to those who have had inadequate mathematics and science in high school. In many states, each year a large fraction of the able students graduate from high school without having had a chance to study physics, or trigonometry, or a modern foreign language.

For example, only 12,000 of the 21,000 senior high schools offer a course in physics. It seems like a hopeless task to find another 9,000 high school physics teachers; indeed, one can argue that we need even more because some of the physics courses offered in the 12,000 schools are not taught by adequately trained teachers. Yet if all the states would proceed with district reorganization and consolidation so that not more than ten per cent of the youth instead of thirty percent were attending small schools, the number of senior high schools might be reduced to something like twelve or thirteen thousand. The problem of providing this number of schools with well-trained physics teachers is by no means a hopeless undertaking. There may well be almost enough such people now teaching physics to man all the high schools of the nation if the citizens would act to eliminate the small high school in most sections of the country.[4]

To a large extent, this present situation is a consequence of the failure of citizens to act. There are areas in the nation, of course, where the population is so widely scattered that it is impossible to have a high school of sufficient size, and in these areas special solutions must be found.[5] But the percentage of the population living in such areas is much smaller than is often thought. Geography is far less of a limiting factor than is often claimed. I know of a school which is serving 3,000 square miles; the pupils come in buses and travel an hour each way. California is not a densely populated state, yet in California ninety-five percent of the youth attending high schools are enrolled in schools of sufficient size — only five percent attend schools with a graduating class of one hundred or less. How much of our academic talent can we afford to waste? This is the question that must be considered state by state. If the answer is "none," then in each state the citizens must discover whether they have done all they can to prevent the waste. In most states this means that the elimination of the small high school through district reorganization and consolidation should have top priority. The state legislature should be urged to pass the necessary laws, the state department of education must provide leadership, and the citizens must respond by reorganizing the high school districts to provide schools of sufficient size. There is no doubt that a drastic reduction in the number of small high schools is possible if citizens desire it. If we really wish to improve public secondary education in the United States in order to meet the national needs in this period of a global struggle, surely district reorganization is a matter of urgency in almost every state in the Union.[6]

Here is one specific set of actions in which citizens could become engaged if they were sufficiently aroused. Yet, with few exceptions, I am not aware of any concerted movement in any state to get forward with this badly needed educational reform. Indeed, in a few states, there are organizations to block any move to reduce the number of small schools. One can only conclude that many people are quite unconscious of the relation between high school education and the welfare of the United States. They are still living in imagination in a world which knew neither nuclear weapons nor Soviet imperialism. They believe they can live and prosper in an isolated, insulated United States. This is true even of some teachers, school administrators, and professional educators who write about public education.

I have met a few professionals who talked as though we were living in the 1930's; they tend to resent any references to the struggle between the free nations and Communism and the consequent existence of a special national interest which ought to affect educational planning. Some teachers and administrators I have met object at once to any line of argument which starts with such phrases as "the nation needs today." Their attention has been centered for so long on the unfolding of the individuality of each child that they automatically resist any idea that a new national concern might be an important factor which should be considered by a parent and a student in planning a high school program. Yet, of course, they would be the first to say that a traditional public concern — education for citizenship —should weigh heavily in the planning of the curriculum. In other words, some of the professional people concerned with public schools seem to me behind the times.

As an example of what I have in mind, let me refer to the resistance to the emphasis on the study of modern foreign languages — a resistance to be found in certain quarters. Few will attempt to justify the existence of courses in foreign languages which run for only two years. Almost all freely admit there is no permanent residue left from this short exposure to a foreign language. The two-year course in Latin, or French, or Spanish (or all three) to be found in so many high schools today is a desiccated residue of what forty years ago was a four-year course. Some parents like a short course, for they can boast that their children have studied a foreign language. Pupils, however, are rarely enthusiastic, for they realize that what is needed is a sufficiently long course so that something approaching a mastery of the language can be obtained. Not many public school officials I have met care to argue strongly for the two-year course of French, for example, but some do question the wisdom of a four-year course. Some would even abandon completely foreign language instruction in the high school. They suggest that Americans just are not interested in learning a foreign language because, unlike Europeans, they will probably never have a chance to use it. This would have been true twenty years ago, before transoceanic airplane service had begun! But with jet planes, it is now a fact that a city in the middle of the United States is nearer London, or Paris, or Rome than those cities were to each other a century ago. Many high school students I have talked to are well aware of this fact. The more able want to study a language long enough to obtain some lasting benefit. These young people know they are living in a new era of transportation. Some of their elders, unfortunately, do not. Of course, part of the blame for the existence of so many two-year courses in high school must rest with the colleges. I have been shocked to discover how many college catalogues state that two years are required or recommended. It would be better to be silent than to encourage high school pupils to study an almost worthless sequence.[7]

The purpose of studying a language is to master it. And for able students something approaching mastery of a modern foreign language can be reached in four years. I am talking about the boy or girl who has the capacity to handle a foreign language. There are many students studying two years of a language who can get nothing out of it and who would get little no matter how long they tried. These students should drop the subject as soon as their lack of talent is clearly indicated. I know that there are some students in many schools whose study of a foreign language is a waste of time. But those who have the capacity should be urged to acquire something approaching a mastery of one modern language by the time they graduate from high school. If they do not, the chances are they never will, and doors are closed to them forever. This is particularly true of boys who are headed for an engineering school. These are able boys who, if properly advised, could and should obtain a command of a foreign language during the high school years. They will rarely have an opportunity to study a foreign language during their years of professional training. At high school it is now or never.

But why, you may ask, should engineers have at least something approaching a mastery of one foreign language? For several reasons, most of which apply likewise to doctors, lawyers, scientists, economists, and other professional people. In the first place, those who do not have a knowledge of another language have a highly restricted view of the way men think. This is particularly true of applied scientists whose professional work concerns quantitative relations of reproducible phenomena. Such people need to realize that some ideas we take for granted may not be readily formulated in another language; it is by no means true that every word or phrase in common use in English has its counterpart in French or German.[8]

But over and above the fact that a knowledge of another language opens a door to another culture, there is a practical reason why our future engineers should learn a foreign language when they are young. This reason is closely related to our struggle with the Soviet Union. In the competition with the Communists in the uncommitted nations of the world, we need to send many engineers as well as other specialists to areas where English is spoken only by a thin layer of the elite and to other places where English is spoken not at all. Those who have traveled in such areas of the world invariably report how successful are the Soviet technicians in dealing with the people as compared to the Americans. They speak the native tongue; Americans do not. But, you may ask, are we to teach Arabic, Iranian, or Indonesian in our schools on the off-chance one of the students may need it? Not at all. The point is this. If a boy has come to know in high school what it means to learn a foreign language, he is in a position to learn a second, a third, or a fourth language with relative ease. The mastery of one foreign language is like passing through a "sound barrier"; once through this barrier the person in question can, in college or later, study effectively the language he needs in a special school. But if a young man who has studied only two years of language in high school attempts this task, he is in an almost hopeless situation. I could document these statements by citing examples of what I have seen overseas.[9]

At this point, let me make it plain that by far the majority of public school administrators with whom I have talked are well aware of the new demands upon the schools. Furthermore, I could name a number of public high schools in which the offerings in foreign languages are adequate and in which a large number of the able students are electing the sort of program which challenges their capabilities to the full. This fact illustrates how impossible it is to generalize about American public secondary education. Anyone who has visited more than a few schools must be aware of the great diversity to be found even within a single state. One set of specifications cannot apply to all high schools because schools should vary in certain respects according to the needs of the communities they serve. I should have to have information about the kind of community the school was serving before I could set up detailed criteria for a satisfactory school.

The road to better schools which I have described in my Report, *The American High School Today*, might be considered merely a widening, straightening, and improvement of the present rather overgrown and winding lane along which most children wander. What I am calling for is immediate action to improve the high school. Without sacrificing what we have gained by providing full-time education for *all* (or almost all) American youth, and without retreating from our belief in the importance of education for citizenship, I believe we can remake our public schools so that they will provide an education suitable for the times in which we live. What we need is to persuade not only certain reluctant educators, but many indifferent parents, that there is a desperate national need for certain types of people with certain highly developed skills. Public school officials, the teachers, and the entire community ought to join in issuing locally a national call to the talented youth to use their school years to develop their talents to the full. Both in terms of their own good and in terms of the welfare of the nation, the case is clear.

Let me postpone until the next chapter a discussion of the type of program an academically talented or highly gifted student ought to be urged to take. Allow me also to postpone a consideration of the role of guidance officers, the requirements for a diploma, and many other important details pertaining to high school education. As I have already indicated, a discussion of American public secondary education makes sense only if one bears in mind the type of community the school in question seeks to serve. And I shall describe later two quite different types of communities and their problems. Furthermore, the remedial measures which must be taken to overcome many of the shortcomings of our high schools (assuming they are of sufficient size) are measures which must be decided locally by the school board and the professional staff. That there is much that a citizen can do at the local level to improve the schools, I hope to demonstrate fully in later pages. In this chapter, I wish to direct attention to problems that are essentially state or national problems and, above all, to urge the importance of establishing a na-

44

tional feeling of urgency which must be the basic driving force for local work.

Is there a danger that, in our worries about technological competition with the Soviet empire, we shall overstress the importance of science and mathematics, propel too large a fraction of our academically talented youth into science, pure and applied? Yes, there is such a danger clearly. But the very diversity of our school pattern and the fact that there are 4000 high schools of sufficient size — almost all of them independent of each other — provide a large margin of safety which otherwise might not exist. There is a real danger, I am certain, of bright boys specializing in mathematics and science in high school to the neglect of the study of English, history, and foreign language. We need engineers who are first-rate engineers (and that means with capacity to handle mathematics); we also need engineers, however, who can write English, who understand human problems, who are broadly educated. And this broad education should start in the high school years.

Are we educating enough engineers or scientists? This is not an easy question to answer, and it is closely related to another equally difficult question — namely: Are we using effectively those who are well trained? As I have traveled around the country, more than one person has spoken about rumors that companies with large government contracts were hiring more engineers and scientists than they, in fact, need. Now I know, from my experience as Deputy Director of the Office of Scientific Research and Development during World War II, how difficult it is to get meaningful information about the use of scientific manpower. I am sure that those in Washington who have the responsibility in these matters are aware of the importance of the effective use of our engineers and scientists. Whether or not new measures should be devised to put more pressure on govvernment contractors to prevent waste of our human resources is a question that might well be considered by some group in the Pentagon.

Those who write alarmingly about our failure to keep pace with the Soviet Union in the output of trained scientists often appear to be sounding a new note of isolationism. Yet only the united free nations can possibly hope to hold in check Soviet ambitions. Let NATO go to pieces, for example, and militarily we are in an exposed and critically dangerous position. But we must not be united just militarily; economically, the free half of the divided world is a unit and must be viable. If another global depression were to take place comparable to that of the early '30's, the Soviets would take over all of Europe; it would be the equivalent of a catastrophic military defeat.

We should think in terms of global strategy, which means thinking in terms of the combined assets of *all* the free nations. Do we do this when we talk about engineers and scientists? Rarely, if at all. I have seen no statements as to the present and predicted future numbers of scientists, pure and applied, in the free world as compared with the Soviet Union and its satellites. Yet these are the figures that are significant, or should be. I say "should be," for we hope those in Washington who are continually struggling to get full cooperation with our allies on the development and manufacture of weapons will succeed.

One may hazard the guess that if our present engineering schools were full to capacity with top-flight students, we would be directing about the right number of able youngsters into careers so vital to the welfare of our highly industrialized nation. But, in addition to those with degrees.

in engineering, we need many highly trained and competent people whose skills are just as vital as the skills of those who sit at a desk all day and figure out calculations. I refer to the vast number who combine manual skills with intellectual skills in a whole spectrum of occupations. The development of new courses in high school for starting boys on careers in such fields as electronics is an educational problem which warrants our attention. So, too, is the expansion of vocational instruction in grades thirteen and fourteen in two-year colleges. I mention these obvious matters because a few of the critics of our public schools who have been vocal in the last fifteen months talk as though they wished to throw out of the high school all vocational courses. To my mind, they are completely wrong. In the high schools I have visited, these courses were of great importance. I know of schools in the suburbs of many cities where, from a national standpoint, it might be desirable to introduce such courses, but the parents will not hear of it. In these suburbs, too many families insist that their children must study only academic subjects and go to college, irrespective of the aptitude of the boy or girl in question. Such families present a problem to counselors, principals, and teachers. To suggest, as some critics of our schools have, that the comprehensiveness of all our high schools be as limited as that of certain suburban schools is to make a suggestion dangerous to the security of our nation.[10]

The nation today needs to mobilize and educate as fully as possible those whose talents will enable them to be professional people and those whose developed skills are indispensable to our highly mechanized society. But an even more fundamental need is the need for an enlightened, public-spirited, and stable electorate and, within each state and each community, men and women who can exercise wise

47

leadership. Every educator is committed to the belief that what happens in our schools and colleges affects to a considerable degree the attitudes of the next generation. With this in mind, in the depression years when Fascism and Nazism were sweeping over Italy and Germany and Communism was winning adherents in France, Americans were primarily concerned with strengthening democracy here at home. Educators were busily discussing ways in which the schools could develop an understanding of our democracy and a loyalty to American traditions. Education for citizenship was spoken of as perhaps the most significant function of secondary education. As a consequence of this effort, almost every competent foreign observer recognizes that we do a better job in the United States in educating *all* our youth for citizenship than does any other nation. Perhaps this is so merely because well over eighty percent of our youth complete at least the first ten grades. But no one should minimize the time and energy that have been devoted to the development of the type of social studies which, it is hoped, will provide an understanding of American democracy. Nor should one ignore the significance of the organization of student activities directed to the same end. We would be foolish, indeed, if we were to discard what has been achieved along the line I have just indicated merely because we were dissatisfied with some aspects of our secondary education.

Too many people, both laymen and educators, tend to put in opposition the education of the future members of the professions and the education of the others. Nothing could be more contrary to the spirit of our American schools and colleges. Under our flexible American system, at least thirty percent of an age group are proceeding with education beyond the high school. Leaders in many walks of life will

48

come from this large group; however, leaders of many communities and many national activities will come from the even larger group who complete their formal education upon graduation from high school. Some people are far too ready to equate the phrase "leading citizens" with the words "professional men and women." Many highly important citizens have not been, and will not be in the future, professional people. Their significance as leaders may develop only in later life and often quite unexpectedly. Unlike some older nations, we are a fluid society, a relatively classless society, and not one in which status is determined once and for all at an early age.

It is because of the importance of leaders of all sorts of organizations that we lay so much stress in our schools on education for citizenship. Each boy or girl in school irrespective of academic ability or vocational goal is not only a future voter, but a potential leader on a local, state, or national level. There is no antithesis between providing a sound general education for *all* American youth and improving the training of the academically talented. Everyone in a good high school receives an academic education aimed at providing the basis for his or her active and intelligent participation in a democratic society. English, history, and the other social studies are the core of such a program. How these subjects are presented to the *entire* student body is of utmost importance to the future of our society. And I have seen excellent work in all these areas.

I think particularly of twelfth-grade classes in the problems of American democracy which I have attended.[11] In these classes, boys and girls with widely different vocational goals and very diverse academic abilities were discussing current political problems and thus learning the ways of democracy. I also found other more direct ways of learning about the

49

democratic process through the use of homerooms and their relation to student councils. In some schools, each room (again a cross section of the school) elected representatives who reported the action of the student council to their constituents (the pupils in the homerooms) and were often subjected to cross examination. I suppose that if I were forced to name one single consequence which I hoped might result from the education for citizenship in our schools, I should say it would be the development of a critical judgment regarding those who were to handle affairs of government.

If our high school graduates have learned to judge shrewdly those who appeal for their votes, they will have learned one of the most important lessons as far as the future welfare of our nation is concerned. This applies to those elected to office at the local, state, and national levels. Because of the nature of the world we live in and the dangers that lie ahead, our future voters need to know enough about international affairs to tell the difference between a windy demagogue and a statesman. We enjoy the benefits of a free country governed by representative government. Vital decisions at the national level cannot be made directly by a citizen. How to develop intelligent discrimination in future voters is one of the most challenging educational questions facing those responsible for the social studies in the high schools of the nation.

I conclude this discussion of the impact of the world situation on public education by returning to the complex and difficult question of federal aid. Does the national need require that Congress annually appropriate large sums for the general support of the public schools in many, if not all, the states? The question is not new. As I indicated in the closing paragraph of the preceding chapter, bills for federal aid for public schools have been introduced into every session of Congress for many years. What is new is the more widespread recognition by national leaders that, because of the grim kind of world in which we live, the nation as a whole cannot be oblivious to the shocking inadequacy of many, many of its schools. Of course, by no means all the inadequacies are a consequence of a lack of money, but I could name community after community where the high school can be made satisfactory only by increasing the expenditure per pupil. And I am referring to schools of sufficient size.

Where is the money to come from? As I explained in the last chapter, the real estate basis for local taxes has proven totally inadequate; in one form or another, funds collected by state taxes are now going to help the local school districts. A number of studies have shown that there is a group of some half-dozen or so states (mostly in the South) in which the resources are insufficient to support adequate schools under any imaginable burden of local and state taxation. Indeed, a number of these states are now taxing the inhabitants more drastically in support of the schools than is the case in most of the richer states. These facts, which have not changed substantially over a period of years, were the basis of the main features of Senator Taft's federal aid bill, which was an equalization proposal combined with a per capita grant for all the states. While the case is strong for using the federal taxing power to syphon some money from the more wealthy states into the coffers of the desperately poor states, the arguments in support of a per capita grant to all the states are far less straightforward. Many who would have supported the equalization feature of the Taft bill (that is, the provision that would have authorized federal money for a relatively few states) were not convinced as to the justice or wisdom of the per capita grant which involved some money flowing to every state.

Since World War II, the proponents of large annual grants of federal money for general support of the public schools have tended to stress the need for funds in all the states. The needs of the few very poor states are not so often underlined.[12] Three basic statements can be made to support the proposition that annually large sums derived from federal income and corporate taxes should be allocated to all (or almost all) states for the general purposes of the public schools. First, there is an overriding national interest in the education of *all* American children; this interest is underlined by population mobility and is more vital than ever before because of our struggle with Soviet imperialism. Second, in all the states there are many school districts which, even if they are large enough, are not performing the educational tasks they should because of lack of money. Third, in almost all states the present arrangement for combining local and state taxes is inadequate because the state is not in a position to allocate sufficient funds. Furthermore, in a number of states, including some of the more wealthy, there is little likelihood that the situation will improve in the immediate future because it appears that the state taxing machinery has been grinding to a halt.

Putting these three statements together, one can conclude that the federal government must use its taxing power to supplement the state taxing power in all or almost all states, so that sufficient money is available at the state capital to assist local districts. It has been proposed that Congress appropriate money directly to the states for the general use of the public schools, the method of distribution within the state to be left to each state to determine. Two questions arise at once. First, leaving aside the dire straits of a few very poor states, what are the chances that without congressional appropriation the states themselves can raise the money for the requisite improvement of the schools? Second, what formula is to be employed in distributing the federal funds, and can such a formula be devised and maintained year by year without the executive branch of the federal government as well as congressional committees becoming heavily involved in public school affairs?

Let me consider the first question. One has to consider the order of magnitude of the sums involved. If the costs per pupil are to remain constant over the next decade, it seems probable that almost all the wealthier states will raise the money to meet the educational needs. These needs would, under this assumption, only correspond to the increased school population. On the other hand, if the costs per pupil should be increased considerably, another situation is at hand. The costs per pupil depend to a large degree on (a) the level of teachers' salaries, (b) the size of the instructional staff. These costs per pupil vary widely from district to district within a state, and the average costs in some states are nearly three times as much as in others.[13] Leaving aside for the moment the question of the level of teachers' salaries, I am sure that higher costs per pupil are required in many schools I have visited because the needed reforms require an increase in the total instructional staff. For example, the number of English teachers should be increased in many instances, so that there is one teacher for every one hundred pupils.[14] The addition of a third and fourth year of a foreign language (needed in so many schools) may necessitate the addition of another foreign language teacher. Rarely do the schools I have visited have enough full-time counselors. With such considerations in mind, I cannot agree with those who conclude that no substantial increase in the cost per pupil is required in many states. On the contrary, my estimate is that a considerable amount of money in almost all states should flow from the state capital to the local districts to supplement the funds raised at the local level.

There can be no doubt as to the necessity for increasing the size of the teaching staff in many schools. Indeed, I am ready to accept the recommendation of the Educational Policies Commission [15] that there should be fifty on the instructional staff for every one thousand pupils in the school system. (This number includes administrators and counselors, as well as classroom teachers.) I am also prepared to argue with anyone as to the necessity of raising teachers' salaries, particularly in certain states. The average salary of the instructional staff in the public schools in 1958–59 was estimated at $4935, and it varied from region to region from a low of $3882 in the Southeast to a high of $5992 in the Far West. New York was the top rate with $6300; Mississippi was at the bottom with $3200. The estimated average salary of classroom teachers was $4775, or 97 percent of the total instructional staff average. About 17.5 percent of the teachers were paid less than $3500; 34.4 percent between $3500 and $4500; 27.9 percent between $4500 and $5500; and 20.2 percent more than $5500. In other words, 80 percent of the classroom teachers were paid less than $5500. [16]

No one can look at such a set of figures and not come to the conclusion that a drastic change in teachers' salaries is needed in at least many states. Such statistics, however, do not tell the whole story. Though a minimum salary scale is often set by the state legislature or the state board of education, the rate of promotion and, hence, the average salary of an instructional staff will vary greatly from one community to another within a state. Moreover, granting that occasionally the salary floor for beginning teachers is competitive with other professions, there is no question that the salary ceiling is much too low, that able college graduates can do better elsewhere in the long run (though some people would challenge this last statement as far as women are concerned). It can be argued that the differences in the cost of living are sufficiently great from one area of the country to another, or even from one town to another within a state, so that some variation in salary scale is to be expected. This may well be so, but this fact does not obscure the need for a great increase in the teachers' salaries in almost all the states. To my mind, each state should answer this question: Is the salary schedule in the state sufficiently high to attract into and hold within the teaching profession able young people in competition with other professions? I believe the answer to this question in almost all states would be an emphatic "no."

Assuming the need for increased instructional staff and a large upgrading of teachers' salaries, we can try and estimate the total national "educational deficit," so to speak, as far as the public schools are concerned. I have seen estimates based on the assumptions that beginning teacher salaries throughout the nation should average $4500 and that the per pupil current expenditure should average at least twelve percent of the beginning salary. Starting with these assumptions, one calculates a per pupil enrolled expenditure of $540 and that at present, the nation over, we should be spending something like eight billion dollars more for our public schools than we are spending.[17] Considering that the present total receipt of state and local governments is thirty-seven billion, the contemplated increase is formidable indeed.[18] The only source of such money, many say, is the federal government. But the annual appropriation by Congress of such a sum of money would represent an increase of nearly ten percent in the federal budget. What is contemplated is the annual appropriation by Congress towards the general maintenance of public schools of an amount somewhat larger than that appropriated in 1958 for the Mutual Security Program and the Atomic Energy Commission combined.[19] To imagine that recurring appropriations of this magnitude can be made without careful budgeting on the part of the administration seems to me to be the equivalent of imagining completely irresponsible government. Careful budgeting will mean, in turn, a strong executive agency which must have access to a mass of factual information about the educational situation in every state. The agency responsible for submitting the annual estimate to the Bureau of the Budget and then supporting the proposals before Congress will have no easy task.

Proponents of a flat grant and various equalization formulas will have to argue their cases from time to time, if not each year. The educational committees of the House and Senate will have every reason to examine into details of curricula and school organization, much as committees of the state legislatures now do from time to time. Certainly, a new chapter in American public education will have opened.[20] It would not be accurate to describe the resulting situation as federal control of our public schools, but we should certainly have a powerful federal influence added to the present influence of the central authority in each state. Whether such federal influence in the long run would be beneficial or detrimental can be argued; much would depend on the tradition which would be developed in the first years of the congressional grant. The one thing that seems to me certain is that at present no one is wise enough to foresee all the consequences of a large annual congressional appropriation to the states for the use of the public schools.

Yet, however fearful one may be of the consequences

of opening the new chapter in public education I have just outlined, it seems to me there is only one other alternative to allowing our schools to remain in their present unsatisfactory situation. That is a radical revision of the tax structure of the states and the federal government. The basic difficulty at present in certain states is that the legislatures, for one reason or another, have refused to pass the necessary tax bills to restore the state finances to a healthy condition. What the proponents of massive federal aid to public education in all or almost all states are saying, in effect, is that because of a breakdown of state political machinery, our schools in many states are suffering. As a consequence, the nation suffers. We must, therefore, use the federal taxing power to raise new money in many states and return this money to the states earmarked for the use of the public schools. Leaving aside the difficulty of finding an equitable formula for the distribution of this money [21] — and the flat grant idea does not recommend itself to me — history shows it will not be easy to persuade Congress to take the required action. Therefore, a thorough exploration of the use in one way or another of the power of Congress to cajole or coerce the states into putting their own financial houses in order seems to me well worth the effort.[22]

In the next decade, one of three things seems to me inevitable. Either our state taxing machinery will have to improve drastically in many states, or Congress will have to start large annual appropriations for public schools, or public education in many states will deteriorate or, at best, stand still at the present unsatisfactory level. If education is as vital to our survival in this deeply divided world as I have portrayed it in this chaper, leaders of opinion throughout the land, to my mind, should be pondering these alternatives.

III

The Citizen's Responsibility

In the first chapter of this volume, I have sketched the governmental framework within which we operate a vast number of tax-supported schools. In the succeeding chapter, I suggested that since we are living in a world quite different from that which existed in the 1920's or 1930's, there is a new national interest in the adequacy of our schools. Because of the nature of our struggle with Soviet imperialism, many Americans feel we can no longer tolerate the kind of education which might have been considered adequate a generation earlier and which is to be found in many schools today. Thousands of high schools do not even offer the kind of instruction which challenges the academically talented students and which is essential for our future professional leaders.[1] To a large extent, this particular inadequacy reflects the attempts of communities to operate high schools that are too small. To cure this situation, as I have pointed out, action by state legislatures is required. The entire citizenry of some states must be awakened to the necessity for radical reform in order that the states in question may not be delinquent in their duty to the nation. In almost all states, further constructive action by the state legislature is required in order to provide an adequate state contribution to the finances of many relatively impoverished districts. Here, as in the case of the reduction of the number of small high schools through consolidation, the voters in the state must be keenly conscious of the national necessity for better schools. Indeed, as I indicated in the concluding pages of the last chapter, the entire body of American citizens must face up to the necessity of either some drastic changes in the federal and state taxing systems or the federal government's becoming involved in public education on a new and very large scale. In short, an American citizen vitally concerned with improving education (as I believe all should be) has opportunities for effective action at both the national and state levels. But perhaps his most immediately effective approach to the problem of providing better schools is as a member of a local community. This chapter, therefore, is addressed to the increasing number of men and women who are anxious to improve their local schools.

The first requisite for such an undertaking is an insight into the problems faced by those who administer a school system. And to obtain an insight one must understand something of the complexities of the American pattern.

To some degree the attention devoted to the shortcomings of our public schools by the media of mass communication in the last few years has tended to confuse the layman. So, too, have the writings of certain critics. The basis of the complaints was hardly new; indeed, to those of us who had been directly involved in education for many years, the stories were quite familiar. What Sputnik accomplished was to provide an attentive audience. Criticism of public education, particularly of the high schools, was good copy. In fact, in the closing months of 1957 and the beginning months of 1958, the more violently a speaker attacked the high school, the more certain he was to have his remarks appear with large headlines on page one.

59

An historian with a sociological bias or a sociologist with historical training could write an interesting article about the sudden burst of highly critical interest in public education which occurred in the fall of 1957. The alarm caused by the military implications of Sputnik was combined with chagrin that the Soviets appeared to have won a scientific race. To the alarm and chagrin was added the impact of reports on Soviet education. By a strange coincidence, highly favorable reports about Soviet education were published almost at the same time as the Russian triumphs in rocketing began to disturb the public mind. To be sure, the news about Soviet education, unlike the reports about Sputnik, did not represent a sudden dramatic turn of affairs. People had been writing for several years about the extraordinarily rapid development of Soviet education; reports on the number of scientists and engineers being educated on the other side of the Iron Curtain had been publicized in the United States in connection with a campaign to encourage more young Americans to study science and engineering. But the publication of an official U.S. Office of Education report on the ten-year schools of the Soviet Union served to dramatize the way the Russians had organized their system of education.[2] Comparisons with American secondary education were quickly made, and the contrast appeared to put the United States schools in a most unfavorable light. All of which provided good ammunition for those who for years had been shooting at the professors of education and the administrators of the public schools.

The future historian of American education will surely ask one question about the episode I have just described. He will wonder why those who were responsible for the tax-supported schools appeared to be so vulnerable to the violent attacks; why the public seemed so ready to believe

the worst about their schools. For years we had been prais-
ing our wonderful system of free schools providing
education for all through the high school and, for many,
through the college years. And then suddenly, as in a fit
of anger, the American public seemed to be repudiating the
whole adventure. I have overdrawn the picture, admittedly,
yet at least one distinguished foreign visitor with whom I
spoke saw the situation much as I have just described it.
"What is the matter with your country?" he inquired.
"Have a couple of Russian rockets set off a panic? You appear to be ready to condemn and throw overboard what
you have bragged about for years — namely, your tax-supported schools. Such talk shakes the confidence of Europeans
in the stability of the American people."

My European friend failed to realize that articulate American opinion, like the wind, comes in violent gusts and may
quickly shift direction. I remember the case of a man named
Dewey, not the philosopher but an admiral, the commander-
in-chief of the U.S. naval forces in the Spanish War. He
was crowned a hero by the American press and a few years
later violently uncrowned. Today, the reputation of a philosopher with the same last name appears to be suffering from
a simliar turn of the wheel of fortune. However, the willing-
ness of citizens to listen to those who have proposed radical
reforms of education cannot be explained solely in terms
of the fickleness of public opinion. There are several deeper
causes. Perhaps the underlying cause is widespread misunderstanding about the nature of the problems facing school
boards and school administrators. To a considerable degree,
I believe this misunderstanding can be dissipated. At all
events, it is one of the purposes of this chapter to make an
effort in that direction.

The lack of understanding is by no means confined to

those who stand outside the teaching profession. Indeed, if the ranks of the educators had presented a solid front, I think the violent critics of public education would have hardly received a hearing. The truth of the matter is that some of the most virulent attacks on the American high schools have come from within the profession itself — from professors in universities. If a citizen hears the public high schools condemned by a professor, he is strongly inclined to believe the professor must be right. The layman may regard professors with suspicion when they talk about politics or economics, but surely a teacher in a university ought to know whether the high schools are good or bad. As a consequence of this attitude, one may encounter a parent who is satisfied with the local high school yet is quite willing to believe the worst about the national situation because he has read an article by Professor X.

University teachers who are highly critical of public secondary education are to be found in the faculties of arts and sciences and in the professional schools, but *not in the schools of education.* In fact, for two generations, in almost every university, there has been little except hostility between the faculty of education and the other faculties. Nearly twenty years ago, I ventured to speak frankly about this matter at the fiftieth anniversary of the founding of Teachers College, Columbia University, and entered a plea for a "Truce Among Educators." [3] At that time, one frequently heard the joke that 120th Street — the east-west street separating Teachers College from the rest of Columbia University — was the widest street in the world. I was told not long ago by one of the younger professors at Teachers College that the street had narrowed perceptibly in the last ten years. I have heard reports from other campuses which point in the same direction. [4] But there is always a time lag in public affairs. If a truce has been finally declared among the educators in some universities, many alumni will probably not yet have heard the news. They may recall only the college years and the way that the English, or history, or chemistry professor used to rail against his colleagues in the school of education.

Nearly five years ago a committee of the American Academy of Arts and Sciences issued a report entitled "On the Conflict Between the 'Liberal Arts' and the 'Schools of Education'." It opens with the sentence, "During the recent past the criticism of our public schools and our institutions for the training of teachers has assumed a degree of vehemence which, whether justified or not, reveals dangerous schisms in the cultural life of the nation." And towards the end of the report, which is largely an excellent historical account of the development of the tensions, the authors state:

"There exists among a considerable number of the defenders of the liberal arts a shocking ignorance of the social problems with which the modern school is confronted. Consequently, these professors attack many of the most well-meant endeavors of our public schools on the basis of inadequate and fallacious criteria. Certainly the capacity of thinking is one of the supreme criteria of man; it can never be sufficiently cultivated. Yet, our modern schools were in no postion to apply this criterion as their exclusive measure of achievement. If they had tried to carry through the program of one of the foremost critics of our high schools and colleges (that every modern citizen 'should understand the great philosophers, historians, scientists and artists'), our whole national life would be in danger of collapse. It would banish into the limbo of ignorance and futility the great majority of this nation, including a considerable number of university instructors. . . .

63

"To repeat: though criticism is needed, there is no salvation in the present fashionable tendency to attack the public school system by the use of incommensurate criteria, forgetting completely that this school system — whatever its obvious defects — has been for about a hundred years the most important instrument in the amalgamation of millions of poor immigrants and native citizens. As a matter of fact, this great achievement has been made possible largely by the use of methods severely criticized by outsiders. Without an attempt at understanding the complexity of a school system which at the same time should fulfill the demands of equality and of quality, of justice and differentiation, of democracy and of an elite within this democracy — and without undergoing the difficult task of relating developments in education to broad changes in our social cultural pattern — without such endeavors on all sides, there can be no productive discussion." [5]

"Without an attempt at understanding the complexity of a school system . . . there can be no productive discussion." I should amend this statement slightly to read as follows: "Without an understanding of the complexities of public education resulting from the diversities of American communities, there can be no productive discussion of the shortcomings of our tax-supported schools." What are the complexities; what are the diversities I have in mind? They are related primarily to those factors influencing American public education which are a consequence of the total social, political, and economic structure of our society — a structure which varies in some significant details from state to state and town to town.

College professors of the liberal arts and many of their friends often discuss school problems as though schools operated in the stratosphere — that is, in a social vacuum. To be sure, it is a convenient fiction to assume all children enter school with the same interests, abilities, preconceived ideas, and return to homes that are culturally identical. It is even more convenient to assume that a community has no interest in a school except as an institution for developing intellectual powers. If one needed an example to illustrate the insufficiency of such premises about education, what is happening south of the Mason-Dixon Line would provide a dramatic case.[6]

It would be easy to multiply examples illustrating what should be the starting point of any discussion about public education — namely, the proposition that the schools in any society operate within the framework determined by that society. Talk about school problems which ignores the framework of society or, by wishful thinking, replaces the real framework with an illusory one at the best is frivolous, at the worst is dangerous. The framework is in part legal, governmental, formal; in part, it is extra-legal, determined by local traditions, customs, by economic and social considerations, and, above all, by family attitudes.

Let me be concrete and ask the reader to go with me in imagination to a high school which I visited not long ago. It is located in a district of a medium-sized city where the rents are low and where, in periods of recession, the unemployment is high. The school is attended primarily by those who live in the district but also by a few who come some distance to enroll in certain of the vocational programs, which have a good reputation. Less than ten percent of those enrolled desire to enter a college on graduation, though more than one four-year institution is located in the city and offers free tuition. Not many more than this small fraction of the student body have the ability to handle satisfactorily the usual twelfth-grade course in physics, trigonometry, or a foreign language. And the more able students (about ten percent) are, for the most part, enrolled in these courses.

The vocational courses are well staffed and well supported and cover a wide range. A girl can go a long way towards becoming an expert in stenography, in office practice work, in running a beauty parlor, in catering and professional cooking; boys on graduation will have completed the equivalent of one year of apprentice work in auto mechanics, airplane mechanics, tool and die work, metal work, and similar trades. All the students, irrespective of their elective programs, are devoting half their time to the improvement of their skill in reading and writing, to the study of some mathematics and science, history, political science, the elements of economics, and to a discussion of current problems. Many, if not all, are benefiting from the courses in art and music and are learning something about the ways of a democracy by the operation of clubs and other extra-curricular activities. The vocational courses for a vast majority represent the vital core of the school program.[7] They represent something related directly to the ambitions of the boys and girls and their parents.

I often wonder if those who inveigh against vocational courses in our high schools have ever visited the kind of school I have just been describing. I wonder if they have ever talked to conscientious teachers in such a school and canvassed the possibility of substituting a sequence of courses in mathematics, chemistry, physics, and foreign languages for the vocational elective programs. If they have and still persist in saying that a school should be concerned only with "mental discipline" or developing intellectual powers, their conclusions have been quite different from my own.

A second illustration of the effect of outside influences on a school and I am through with my examples of community diversity. Again, let me take the reader on an imaginary journey to visit a school I know which is by no means unique, either in its setting or its organization. It is located in an area of the type which is usually referred to as a high-income residential district. The families who send their children to this school have very different ambitions for their offspring from those of the families living in the city school district I first described. There are no skilled workmen who wish their sons to follow in their footsteps. Most of the parents are professional people; almost without exception they assume their children must go to college. Some are very specific about the college the boy or girl must enter. And, if the college in question is highly selective in its admission policy, grief and frustration in the senior year may be in store for all concerned unless a wise counselor recognizes in the lower grades the limitations in academic ability which no amount of study can overcome, or recognizes that, even if perfectly acceptable, the boy or girl in question may not be accepted because of the limited size of the college freshman class.

In part as a result of the cultural habits of the parents, the number of slow readers in this school is smaller than in the other school I just portrayed; the fraction of the student body who can effectively handle mathematics and a foreign language is much larger.[8] Nevertheless, a considerable number of the boys and girls have the greatest difficulty with eleventh- and twelfth-grade mathematics and science and can progress only very slowly in the study of a foreign language. In these cases, parental ambition often outruns student ability. As a result, in this school there is an experienced counselor whose full-time job it is to locate colleges with sufficiently low standards to admit even those who, in terms of national norms of scholastic aptitude, are in the third quarter of the high school population. Over the years, this counselor has been most successful.[9]

I might note parenthetically that one of the factors leading to the present highly vocal discontent with public education has been the increasing demands of parents in certain suburbs for a purely academic curriculum for all their children. A generation ago the equivalent of many of these families would have sent their children to private schools. The income tax and a greater number of children have forced more than one family to rely on public education as the means of getting a son or daughter into a particular college. Thirty years ago a similar family would have turned to a private boarding school or day school which had the reputation of being a good college-preparatory school. In those days colleges were not overburdened with applicants; the admission policies were such that a boy or girl with less than average academic ability, by hard work and skillful coaching, could pass the necessary subject-matter examinations and eventually accumulate the necessary credits for admission. I need not stress how different the highly selective admission policies of many colleges are today. The trouble in some suburban communities is that the parents are still thinking in terms of the colleges of their youth. They may demand that the school accomplish the impossible — namely, transform a boy or girl with little academic talent into a brilliant pupil; and, if frustrated by the actual situation, they are only too ready to blame the superintendent, or the principal, or the school board, or probably all three.

To be intelligent about his local situation, a citizen must assess to some degree the needs of the community in regard to vocational education. He has to make an effort to see the schools as serving the children of all the families, not just his own and his friends' children. An important clue to vocational needs is the percentage of high school graduates who, year after year, enter an institution of higher learning. Clearly, there is not much demand for vocational courses in the suburban school I just described because of the large fraction of students going on to college. In regard to specific vocational offerings, one must know the kinds of jobs available to those who wish to go to work full time immediately on graduation, for vocational work in high school must be related to employment possibilities.[10] Whether or not local opportunities for part- or full-time education in a two-year college are available is another matter of great importance, because the relation of the community college (if one exists) to the high school may affect to some degree the organization of the high school work, especially in vocational areas.[11] In short, a variety of questions must be answered before a citizen is in a position to discuss the highly controversial subject of the extent and kinds of practical and vocational courses (if any) which should be included in the curriculum of the high school.

Whatever may be a citizen's considered opinion, after careful study, as to the need for more or fewer vocational offerings in the local high school, he is almost certain to have strong opinions about the nonvocational work. He will have read so much about the failure of the American high schools to challenge the able student that he is on the alert to discover whether or not the criticism is valid in his own hometown.

First, one must ascertain the course offerings in the high school. For example, is it possible for a student to pursue the study of a foreign language for four years?[12] Are twelfth-grade courses in mathematics, physics, and chemistry available every year? (There are many small high schools in which this is not the case.) Second, a constructive critic of the school system ought to know the minimum requirements for a high school diploma. To my mind, they should include the study of English each of four years, the study of social studies for at least three of the four years, and at least one year each of mathematics and natural science. Third, one should try to find out whether the students who have the ability to carry courses in advanced mathematics, science, and a foreign language as well as in English and social studies are, in fact, electing such a full academic program. Not until a person is in possession of at least this much information is he in a position to pass even a first judgment on a school system.

The third item I have just listed presents difficulties, for, unlike the first two, such information is usually not available. This fact I discovered in connection with my study of the comprehensive high school to which I have already referred so often. Without some knowledge of what kinds of students are electing what sorts of courses, one cannot make meaningful statements about a school. Every school board, I believe, should ask the superintendent to request the high school principal to prepare an academic inventory of each graduating class. Each student's actual program for four years, together with a measure of his or her potential academic ability as measured by a scholastic aptitude test, should be recorded on a card.[18] The individual cards with the students' names should be kept highly confidential, of course. But a summary of the results should be published each year. Since tests of mathematical and verbal aptitude given in the lower grades are a rough measure of each student's potentialities, the published summary should show what percentage of the potentially abler students had elected various sequences of courses. For example, in one high school from which I obtained an academic inventory, at least half the boys whose test scores placed them in the top fifteen percent of the high school population on a national basis (the academically talented) had elected four years of mathematics, three years of science, and four years of foreign language, on top of the required four years of English and three years of social studies. By way of contrast, in another school far fewer than half the boys in the same category had elected as much as four years of mathematics, just over a half had elected as much as three years of science, and only a small percentage had studied a foreign language more than two years.[14] I have referred to the programs of boys only because under our present social mores engineering, science, and medicine are almost exclusively male preserves. It is a pity that more able girls are not electing science and mathematics in school and college, for careers are open in teaching and research, at least, for capable women well trained in these subjects.

The making of an academic inventory does not commit a school board to a policy concerning what the potentially able boys and girls ought to study. Yet I think the school board might well adopt a policy in this regard to serve as a guide to the counselors. And I think as a minimum program for the academically talented (the top fifteen percent on a national basis) the board should have in mind the following: four years of English, three years of social studies (including two of history), three years of science, four years of mathematics, and four years of one foreign language. For the academically talented boys, at least, I feel this is a minimum program. With a seven- or eight-period day, there is room for art and music too. For girls, perhaps, a second foreign language might be substituted for twelfth-grade mathematics or science, but for the boys *in this group,* a second foreign language, I believe, should be in addition to what I have just listed.

To my mind, in every school the guidance officers, who play such a vital role in a nonselective comprehensive school, should urge every pupil whose scholastic aptitude test scores and work in the lower grades indicate academic talent to start a four-year mathematical sequence and a four-year foreign language sequence. If the boy or girl in question really cannot handle the one subject or the other by the time the eleventh grade is reached, then a more restricted elective program may be in order. However, I believe the presumption should be that a student whose test scores in the eighth grade place him in the upper fifteen percent of the high school population on a national basis is capable of studying a wide academic program effectively and rewardingly. In other words, if he is academically talented, he should develop his talents as fully as possible while he is young.

The real issue will not often be an issue to be settled by the school board or the administrative officials — it will be a community issue. How hard do the parents of the able children want their children to work? To what degree will the community support the efforts of a school board to urge the academically talented to take a wide program? In many a school I have been in, the more able boys and girls complained they could not devote as much time to study as they wished because their evenings were taken up by activities arranged by organizations in the community. If the leading citizens in such cities really sense the realities of the kind of world in which we live, they will be the first to say to the bright boy or girl, "For your own sake and for the sake of the nation, do your homework."

Anyone familiar with the facts about the high school population will recognize that it is impossible to have one standard academic curriculum for all pupils. That is, it is impossible if high standards in mathematics, science, and foreign languages are to be maintained. Of course, one can require that even pupils with very little academic ability be *exposed* to such subjects, but for a high school student to profit from the exposure he or she must have a certain minimum of ability and be prepared to work. The accumulated experience of countless teachers demonstrates that the profitable study of mathematics beyond elementary algebra or the study of a foreign language with the objective of mastery is just too difficult for certain pupils. For others, such study is relatively easy, and these are the pupils who should be urged to study these subjects. For an intermediate group — and the line between this group and the academically talented is hazy — much will depend on the attitudes of the boy or girl and the parent. What the educators call "motivation" is for this group all important. No one should attempt to be dogmatic about the size of this intermediate group or the elective programs they should study. Given sufficient ambition, many a pupil whose academic talent is not very great may, by hard work, be able to keep up with his more brilliant classmates in both mathematics and foreign languages. But there are limits to what even hard work can accomplish, as every teacher knows. Any realistic appraisal of the problems of secondary education results in the conclusion that there must be a wide variety of courses in the high school.

All right, the reader may ask, if not all pupils can handle a tough academic program, why not require just the bright students to take the tough courses? To this I would reply: How? There is no way in a free country by which organized society can *require* bright children to study hard. One can imagine a school assigning all the pupils with an I.Q. above a certain score to a prescribed, stiff program of academic studies, yet what if the students refuse the challenge and do not do the work? Drop them from the program? This would keep up standards, but the over-all objective would not have been accomplished. The chances are that the arbitrary assignment of pupils to such a program would cause resentment from some of those who were included as well as considerable pressure from parents whose children were excluded. As a matter of fact, I can hardly conceive of a community agreeing to any such arbitrary and deterministic scheme. Some high schools do attempt to solve the problem by setting up a special academic track with a prescribed course of study that a student may *elect*. However, there is no way of insuring that all the able students will choose the program and do the work; the decision of the student largely depends on the attitudes of the parents and counselors and the spirit of the school. Even if, in place of a special academic program within a high school, one established a series of special selective academic high schools (a radical innovation which would take much time), there would be no guarantee that any large fraction of those who ought to attend would, in fact, enroll.[15] The more one studies the problem of how to develop academic talent through education in a free society, the more one concludes that attempts at compulsion are not the answer. A climate of opinion must be created which brings forth in each young person a strong desire to do his or her best in school. Then the schools must, in turn, provide the challenging courses and provide a variety so that not only the academically talented student but every student will feel his studies are worthwhile.

I have been discussing the necessity for advanced mathe-

74

matics, science, and foreign languages on an *elective* basis. English and social studies, on the other hand, are *required* and are presented to all or almost all high school students irrespective of their talents. It would require a long discussion to go into the basic reasons why the study of English or history is different from the study of mathematics beyond elementary algebra, or physics, or the study of foreign language. One illustration may suffice. Almost all pupils can achieve a certain degree of competence in English composition, though the quality of the themes written, even with the best instruction, will vary enormously. Everyone agrees that one of the objectives of a high school is to improve the writing ability of every child. The poorest writer should be able to write a simple letter, while the best may be trying his or her hand at poetry. Contrast this with the study of trigonometry. Unless the student can reach a certain level of understanding and skill in handling the concepts and symbols, nothing has been accomplished by the course of study. A certain absolute level of competence must be soon reached or the rest of the course is meaningless. So, too, with other mathematical courses usually given in grades ten, eleven, and twelve; so, too, with the study of foreign languages or physics as given in grades eleven or twelve. On the other hand, the social studies courses at the high school level are like English.

I have devoted considerable attention to the kind of student who has certain talents which, when properly developed, lead to academic skills. It is interesting that we have been quite ready to recognize other kinds of talents — not only to recognize them but to stress the value of the skills that can be developed from them. I refrain from overelaborating on our interest in athletic talent! One reason for public recognition of this particular talent is the fact that it is easily observable. Artistic and musical talents likewise are readily discernible. For this reason, and because of the long-term benefits to the individual that come from the development of musical and artistic skills, much time and money have been devoted to instruction in these fields in our public schools. As a people, we have been increasingly concerned with raising the cultural level of the country.

Until very recently the American public has shown little interest in academic ability or the manipulative talents of skilled workmen. Yet, recalling the Biblical parable, we should not bury these talents but rather develop them. If a basketball coach sees a boy over six feet tall with good coordination, he will urge the boy to try out for the basketball team. The same principle should hold true for students with academic or manipulative talents; they have certain potential skills that should be developed. Further, just as the American public has the good sense to realize that success in basketball means a combination of special talent and good coaching, so we should recognize that success in these other areas means talent combined with good teaching. Both are needed.

I pointed out in the preceding chapter that the assumption that all leaders and good citizens in society will come from the academically talented group is utterly false. It is true that most of the professional people — doctors, lawyers, engineers, scientists, and scholars — are recruited from this group. But just as one cannot possibly say that good citizens are people with basketball skills, so one cannot say that good citizenship is tied directly to skills resulting from the study of foreign languages or advanced mathematics and science.

How, then, do our schools promote what we might call the skills of good citizenship? It is my belief, as I stated earlier, that the general education required of all students, regardless of special talents, academic or otherwise, serves

76

this purpose. The ability of students to participate in our free society as active and effective citizens will be developed by a required program in English (four years). social studies (at least three years), and some mathematics and science, together with the various out-of-class activities that mark a comprehensive high school. These courses and activities are designed to develop in every student his or her power of reasoning, as well as an understanding of our cultural heritage, the traditions of our society, and the give-and-take of democracy in action. It should go without saying that we must do all we can to protect this vitally important function of our schools.

One question which troubles many parents and many citizens who are not parents of children now in school is the following: How do we know, even if all the pupils are required to study certain subjects (such as English) for a period of years, that they will benefit from the instruction? How can we be sure, even if all the academically talented boys elect twelfth-grade mathematics and four years of a foreign language, that these students will have their talents in these fields developed to the full? In other words, what guarantees can we have that the quality of the teaching in a school is adequate?

This is an important question, and it highlights the obvious fact that good teachers are essential at every stage of our educational system. Yet, with the salary schedule what it is in most states, it is difficult to see how we are going to recruit each year a sufficient number of able young people to provide the teachers that we need. Therefore, every citizen concerned with the quality of the teaching in his schools might well be concerned with the level of the teachers' salaries.

When it comes to assessing the performance of any individual teacher, a layman should proceed with the utmost caution. Excellent teachers are usually well known and recognized in a community after a period of years. But the crucial question of determining the potentialities of a teacher on trial is not a question for outsiders to take a hand in. Only professionals with experience (particularly the superintendent and principals of the schools) are in a position to weigh all the evidence which must be considered in determining whether a teacher should be made a permanent member of the staff. The judicious use of standard achievement tests and examinations enables the administration of a school system to follow the work of various teachers, and I know of a number of schools in which such devices are constantly and wisely used. In the final analysis, the quality of the teaching depends on the skill of the administrators in recruiting the staff and providing inspiring leadership.

The last point needs underlining, for good teachers will not teach well in a system where the morale of the staff has been destroyed by unwise actions of the school board or its agents. The community should have confidence in the school board, the superintendent, and the other administrative officers. In other words, they should have confidence in the management's ability to obtain good teachers and stimulate them to do their best. And I should like to conclude this brief discussion of the key role of the teachers by stating that I have visited many high schools with a good reputation and found this reputation justified by the quality of the teachers I have met.

The title of this chapter indicates my conviction that a heavy responsibility rests on each citizen for the improvement of our schools. Let me sum up what can be done at the local level. The citizen who wishes to do his part should, first of all, orient himself to the complexities of the task we have assigned our public schools. Second, he should get the facts about the current local situation. Then, armed with this knowledge, he is in a position to be part of a constructive force. Depending on the circumstances of the time and place, he may wish to help organize a local citizens committee in support of the public schools.[16] He certainly will do all in his power to see to it that responsible, intelligent, public-spirited citizens are candidates for election to the local school board, and in the recurring public discussion of the financing of the schools he will be ready to support energetically the school board's recommendations, provided, of course, that he has become convinced of their soundness. And in order to become convinced he will, together with other citizens, be supplied by the school board with answers to a great variety of pertinent questions. In addition to knowing the requirements for a diploma, the course offerings, and the results of an academic inventory of each graduating class, he may wish to inquire as to the instruction in English composition. Are the teachers overloaded and, therefore, not in a position to give adequate attention to theme writing? (They are in many schools that I have visited.) Are the standards for passing an elective academic course kept sufficiently high, or has community pressure caused the superintendent to let it be known that the teachers must be careful not to fail too many? (I could name schools where this situation exists and where, as a consequence, the less able students are being deceived by thinking they have learned something about a foreign language, for example, when in fact their accomplishment is almost nil.) What, if anything, is being done for the highly gifted student (a small percentage of the population)? Such students are apt to be bored even by academic courses suitable for an academically talented boy or girl. A number of high schools are providing opportunities for these extremely able students to anticipate one or more freshman college courses in their senior high school year.

As I pointed out in the preceding chapter, there are something like four thousand high schools in the United States that are large enough to be able to provide adequately for the whole spectrum of abilities and interests to be found in the usual American community. Many of these, as I know from visits to them, are unsatisfactory in one or more respects. Some, as I judge from hearsay, are extremely inadequate in regard to the education of the more able students. Yet the faults could be remedied in almost all the instances with which I am familiar by relatively minor changes, assuming, of course, that money for the improvements is available. The conclusion of my study of the American comprehensive high school has been, therefore, that we need no radical change in the basic pattern, except as regards the schools that are too small.

Now I know that there are critics of our public schools who disagree with any such statement. These "radical reformers," as I call them, are apt to base their arguments on the alleged superiority of European schools. I happen to know something about the schools in Germany and also about those in Switzerland by first-hand observation. I also know something about the schools in France, though only indirectly. The references to European education I read in the papers lead me to believe that there is a widespread misunderstanding in the United States about this subject.[17] Therefore, I venture to conclude this chapter by answering a question I sometimes hear — namely: Would it not be a good idea to import the European system of education into the United States?

People who incline to answer this question offhand in the affirmative have usually had experience with one type of European school — the German *Gymnasium* (or *Oberreal-schulen*) or the French *lycée*. These schools, which one may conveniently designate as pre-university schools, enroll not more than a fifth of an age group; the selection of those enrolled is made at ten to eleven years of age. The other four fifths of the youth, with a few exceptions, complete their full-time education at age fourteen and go to work. The course of study in the pre-university schools is far from easy. The homework is heavy; standards are high; often as many as two thirds fail during the eight- or nine-year course. Those who succeed then take a national examination and receive a certificate that admits to any university. (I am speaking here of Germany and Switzerland.) There is no equivalent of the four-year liberal arts college in all of Europe. The pre-university school provides all the general or liberal education that the future university student will receive. A European university is the equivalent of our graduate professional schools — law, medicine, arts and science.

One may find the education obtained in the European pre-university schools excellent in many respects, as I do with certain reservations, and yet realize that the way this education is given in Europe is literally impossible in the United States. Let us see what would be required to Europeanize American education. First of all, one would have to abolish all the independent liberal arts colleges (over 1000 rugged institutions — quite a job). Second, one would have to eliminate or greatly alter large areas of instruction in many universities. Third, one would have to set up a uniform examination for admission to the universities and uniform standards for degrees. Fourth, one would have to change the laws on employment of youth and the school-leaving age and correspondingly persuade labor unions and management to imitate the European practice in regard to employment of young people. And last, but by no means least, one would have to abolish local school boards and place the control of the curriculum and the employment of teachers (including their allocation to a specific school) in the hands of the government of each state.

But what would be even more difficult than all this re-organization would be a necessary reversal of the whole trend of developments in our history. One would have to persuade the people of this country to turn their backs on those characteristics of our society which are a product of our special history and which, formulated as ideals, have guided so many generations. One would have to modify profoundly the American belief in local responsibility and the American attachment to two ideals derived from our frontier history — the ideals of equality of opportunity and the equality of status of all forms of honest labor.

Anyone who wishes to take on seriously a reform movement to bring about any one of the changes I have listed is welcome to the job. To my mind, he wouldn't get to first base, nor should he. As I have already indicated, I am convinced we can develop the talents of all our youth without any basic changes in the pattern of secondary education, provided that, state by state and community by community, the citizens will do their part. Public awakening to the necessity for improvement in the light of our struggle with the Soviet Union is the first step, but alone this is not enough. Citizens in each city and town must get the facts about the local schools and then be prepared to go to work. A first-rate school board must be elected and then supported in its efforts to improve the schools.[18] The road to better schools will be paved by the collective action of the local citizenry in thousands of communities. The responsibility for the sorely needed upgrading of our schools cannot be passed to the state legislatures or to Congress. The responsibility rests on every citizen in the land.

❧ IV ❧

The Revolutionary Transformation of the American High School

In the preceding chapters I have referred more than once to the revolutionary transformation of the American public school which occurred between 1905 and 1930. Although I have postponed until this last chapter a consideration of the details of this bit of American history, I believe a failure to be aware of the events which constitute the story is a major block to an understanding of the present situation, and I believe there has been widespread ignorance among laymen about what actually happened to youth in the United States in the first three decades of this century. According to my interpretation of the last fifty years, the American public between 1930 and 1945 was so concerned with first the Depression and then a global war that few laymen fully realized that a revolutionary transformation of the schools had just occurred. Only after the post-war adjustment had been made did any large number of articulate Americans wake up to what had happened. And as often is the case with those suddenly awakened from a deep sleep, the first exclamations were not too closely related to the actual situation.

In 1905 something like a third of the children who first enrolled in grade one entered a high school (grade nine).

Only about nine percent of an age group graduated from high school, and only four or five percent of an age group entered college. In 1930, instead of only a third of the youth entering high school, well over three-quarters were registered in the ninth grade; instead of nine percent graduating, almost forty-five percent of an age group finished high school; and the college entries had risen from five percent of an age group to about fifteen percent. It is interesting to note that while the percentage attending college increased, the percentage of high school graduates going on for further education declined because of the greater increase in high school enrollment.

In 1905, the curriculum of almost all public high schools was academic; the country over, half the pupils in grades nine to twelve were studying Latin. Few if any schools, except manual training schools, were offering courses involving senior shopwork for boys; few girls were studying, at taxpayers' expense, stenography, domestic economy, or bookkeeping; little, if any, time was devoted to art and music. By 1930 the widely comprehensive high school was to be found in many sections of the country; boys and girls were spending as much as half their time in grades eleven and twelve on courses designed to develop skills marketable on graduation; the art and music departments were expanding rapidly; Latin was disappearing from the curriculum except for a two-year course. Institutions of higher education, both private and public, were enrolling students whose only academic credential was a high school diploma, and by 1930 this often meant the graduate had a minimum exposure to those academic subjects considered essential twenty-five years before.

How and why did the revolutionary change occur? To read some accounts, one would think that a band of professors of education had decided that for the future well-being of our society it was essential that all American youth stay in school full time through grade twelve. Therefore, they enlisted the teachers, as in a crusade, and persuaded the state legislators to raise the age of compulsory attendance to force the boys and girls to stay in school. They then proceeded to focus attention on education for citizenship and understanding the ways of democracy. The high school curriculum was revolutionized to correspond to this new approach, and a host of elective courses was provided to take care of the wide spectrum of abilities and interests in the high school population, which was now to include *all* the youth of a city, town, or district. According to those who see the revolution in the way I have just described, John Dewey's *School and Society*, first published in 1899, and his *Democracy and Education*, published in 1916, were the inspiration and guide for the educational crusade.

Quite a different account might run as follows: The transformation in methods of production which we talk so much about today had already started in the first decade of this century; apprentice training, characteristic of Europe, was disappearing; the land-grant colleges were making the farmers conscious that going to college might have practical value, and, therefore, it was worth while for a boy to finish high school in order to get to college. A vigorous humanitarian movement to abolish child labor was getting under way; Congress in 1916 passed a law prohibiting child labor. Though the federal law was declared unconstitutional, the momentum of the movement to abolish child labor was far from lost. State laws were passed regulating the employment of young people. A demand for vocational education grew rapidly; it was backed by factory owners, farmers, and labor leaders, and resulted in the passage of the Smith-Hughes Act in 1917, which appropriates federal funds for vocational education. These social, economic, and legal changes, taken together with an attitude of some labor leaders who were anxious to restrict rather than expand the number of applicants for jobs, forced many young people to stay in school. A generation earlier, the same type of youngster would have gone to work at fourteen or even younger. As a consequence, from 1905 to 1930 the schools from grades six to twelve were filling up with types of pupils different from those the teachers had known before. The teachers appealed to the professors in the teachers' colleges for help. Their cries of distress were answered by such writings as John Dewey's volume of 1916 and the *Cardinal Principles of Secondary Education*, published in 1918 by a Commission of the National Education Association. In short, according to this second view, it was the change in the employment picture which forced parents to keep their children in school, irrespective of their academic talent and their desire to go to college. This change in the nature of the high school population, in turn, forced the school administrators, teachers, and educational theoreticians to accommodate the high schools to the new order.

I have purposely sketched two extreme interpretations of an educational transformation. The first puts the educators triumphantly in the driver's seat; the second depicts them as conscientious public servants trying to do their best to solve problems not of their own making. One may be quick to say that the truth lies somewhere in between these two extremes and, furthermore, that an analysis of this past episode in American education is of interest only to historians. But, as to this last point, I would disagree. The nature of the transformation of the high school bears directly on the current discussion of the shortcomings of American public secondary education. I have read accounts of the revolution in American education which come very close to the interpretation I first put forward. In such accounts, the raising of the school-leaving age is the one legal sanction, so to speak, which the reforming educators required to forward their ambitions toward universal education of American youth. And more than one layman has accepted at face value this account of the revolution which the educators claim was theirs. Some laymen, perhaps the great majority, have applauded the revolution, but in recent years some have had grave misgivings. Not a few have said: "If the professionals can persuade the legislators to raise the school-leaving age, why can't some of us get together and lower it?" Continuing the argument, such laymen are apt to say: "There are a lot of boys and girls in high school today who have no business being there; they haven't the interest or ability to benefit from what a school ought to be concerned with, namely, training and nourishing the mind. Let's change the laws on compulsory school attendance and get back to where we were in the first decade of this century."

Some such statements have been made to me more than once in the last two years. Implicit in the point of view thus expressed is the notion that the revolutionary transformation of the high school was a social change which, like prohibition, could be reversed. One pressure group succeeded in amending the Constitution to prohibit the sale of liquor, and a second succeeded later in nullifying this amendment by the adoption of still another. Thus a new social situation which in the 1920's appeared to many to be permanent turned out to be only temporary. If one clock, prohibition, could be turned back, why not another, namely, education; so argue privately some educational counter-revolutionists.

Is the change in the educational pattern which occurred between 1905 and 1930 comparable to the change brought about by the prohibition amendment, or is it more like the changes in our methods of transportation which occurred in about the same period of time? Both transformations — the one affecting the drinking habits of the American public, the other the habits of locomotion — were the result of free decisions. That is to say, no dictator, no occupying power, promulgated decrees or put the force of the state to work to modify our habits. Clearly, the first change — prohibition — could be reversed by a change of law, but equally clearly the second cannot; a successful counter-revolution affecting traffic would require a reorientation of a complex social pattern. Only a person bereft of reason would undertake to get state legislatures or the federal Congress to pass laws limiting drivers' licenses or raising gas taxes so that, as a consequence, the ratio of persons to cars would be what it was in 1910. For those who are radically dissatisfied with the basic premises of our present educational system, the question to consider is the following: Was the transformation of 1905–1930 comparable to prohibition or to the change in our methods of transportation? In short, is it or is it not a reversible social process?

For those who are at all familiar with the employment picture in the United States, to ask this question is to answer it. Nevertheless, I venture to remind the reader of a few facts of history which I find some contemporary critics of American public education sometimes seem to overlook. The first is the success of the movement to abolish child labor — a success which came only gradually to be sure; the second is the alteration of the attitude of labor leaders and management towards the employment of young people; the third is the continuous change in the nature of the demand for labor, a constant increase in the ratio of skilled to unskilled jobs; the fourth is the disappearance of the apprentice system as it existed in 1900 and still exists on the Continent of Europe. Taking the country as a whole, we find in 1910 that thirty percent of the youth fourteen and fifteen years of age were employed; by 1930 the figure had dropped to nine per cent; for the sixteen- and seventeen-year-olds, the employment figure for 1910 was sixty-six percent; by 1930 it had dropped to thirty-two percent. The school enrollment of both groups had correspondingly increased.

To be sure, it was only in the days of the New Deal that national laws regulating child labor were passed that were not subsequently declared unconstitutional (the Walsh-Healy Public Contracts Act of 1936 and the Fair Labor Standards Act of 1938). But in many heavily industrialized states, the new pattern had been established before Franklin Roosevelt took office. One has only to contrast the present European and American practices in the teaching of skilled mechanics to see what happened in this country in this century. In Germany today, those who are to become skilled workers in metal start their apprentice work at age fifteen in a school run by a large industrial concern; they also attend a few hours each week a continuation school run by the state. In the United States, in some communities, the first year of apprentice work may be anticipated by vocational courses in grades eleven and twelve (under the Smith-Hughes Act) either in a vocational high school or a widely comprehensive high school. But apprentice training on the job rarely starts before a boy is seventeen or eighteen years of age.

Let me make it plain that in stressing the alteration in the employment scene I do not mean to imply that the educators had no influence on the transformation of the high school. The true interpretation of the revolutionary transformation of secondary education lies between the two extremes I earlier depicted. Professors of education and public school administrators were in part responsible for the changes which occurred. But so, too, were labor leaders, the humanitarian reformers seeking to abolish child labor, certain industrialists. and the innovating engineers who were altering the nature of industrial processes. So, too, in fact, were professors of the liberal arts who, when they saw the population of the public high schools altering, decided to leave the study of the new pedagogic problems to the professors of education.[1] It is impossible to assay the relative contributions made by the professional educators acting directly on the content of the high school curriculum and the other group — labor leaders, humanitarian reformers — whose ideas and actions changed the framework within which the high school teachers had to operate. Chronologically, the two groups were simultaneous in their actions; as each decade passed, the results of their efforts reinforced each other.

As evidence in support of my somewhat dogmatic assertions about the changes in the composition of the high school student body, let me quote from an influential educator who was writing in 1917 — a year which falls halfway in the revolutionary period 1905–1930. The educator I have in mind is Alexander Inglis. In his *Principles of Secondary Education*, published in 1918, Professor Inglis writes about the "noteworthy changes [which] have taken place in the secondary school population." This population, he declares, has changed in the course of twenty-five years from "a roughly homogeneous group of those designed for the higher walks of life to a highly heterogeneous group of pupils destined to enter all sorts of occupations." [2] The causes of the change, which is referred to more than once in the volume, were primarily social and economic. But on one important point it seems clear that the educational reformers (of whom Inglis was an outstanding leader) had already had influence on the composition of the student body of the high schools and soon would have still more. A decade earlier, it had been widely accepted practice to restrict admission to a four-year high school to those who had satisfactorily completed the work of the first eight grades. As a consequence of this practice, a considerable number of students were repeating the work of the lower grades, and not a few were leaving school without even having entered high school. With the introduction of the junior high school, which was taking place at the time Professor Inglis wrote, rigid separation of the high school from the lower grades was broken down; furthermore, promotion by subject, rather than by grades, was being advocated. One judges that, by 1917, it was far less common to find a sizeable fraction of the fifteen-year-olds in grade eight or lower. Just how widely what is now called "social promotion" had been adopted, I cannot say, and Professor Inglis' recommendation cannot be so classified. But it seems probable that an educational reform designed to correct a situation that found some young people two or three years older than their classmates had increased the heterogeneity of the high school population.[3]

Reading Professor Inglis' volume in the light of what has happened since was to me a fascinating experience. One saw a revolution through the eyes of a revolutionary, one might almost say, or at least a reform through the eyes of a reformer; one noted the current appraisal of those social changes that made imperative certain pedagogic reforms. But, in addition, one reads an account of a process which was still going on and learns what the progressive educators at the time of World War I were predicting about the future. Reading the 1918 Report of the NEA Commission on the Reorganization of Secondary Education affords something like the same experience, yet, since the Report is brief, the argumentation is kept to a minimum. Professor Inglis was a member of the NEA Commission and, I judge, an influential member. Certainly his book and the Report agree on all essential points.

The NEA Report to which I have been referring is generally known by its title, *Cardinal Principles of Secondary Education*. There seems no doubt it has had, and still continues to have, a profound influence on the way public school people have formulated their problems and endeavored to explain to the public what they were accomplishing. Those who are primarily interested in the formulation of educational principles and pedagogic theories have centered their attention on the cardinal principles themselves. Such people are concerned to trace the influence of the progressive movement in education, which had started in the 1890's, on the principles and their elaboration by the NEA Commission.[4] The mood in which I am writing is one which, as I explained at the outset, is not congenial to educational theorizing. So, I may be forgiven if I skip over a large segment of the orthodox treatment of American educational history with only a single comment on the role of progressive education in the revolution I am considering in this last chapter. As I read the NEA Report, Professor Inglis' volume, and the writings of John Dewey before 1920, I am struck with the way the new ideas fit the new problems as a key fits a lock. Confronted with a "heterogeneous high school population destined to enter all sorts of occupations," high school teachers and administrators and professors of education needed some justification for a complete overhauling of a high school curriculum originally designed for a homogeneous student body. The progressives with their emphasis on the child, "on learning by doing," on democracy and

93

citizenship, and with their attack on the arguments used to support a classical curriculum were bringing up just the sort of *new* ideas that were sorely needed. After closing John Dewey's volume, *Democracy and Education*, I had the feeling that, like the Austro-Hungarian Empire of the nineteenth century, if John Dewey hadn't existed he would have had to be invented. In a sense perhaps he was, or at least his doctrines were shaped by the school people with whom he talked and worked.

I have touched so far only on how the past and current scene appeared to Inglis and his colleagues — what I might call the first half of the transformation. Let us now examine their views about the future. It seems quite evident that they failed to realize in 1918 how rapidly the change in the high school population was taking place and how far it would go within another decade. At the time they were writing, the number who left school after completing only grades seven or eight was still large. The NEA Commission says of such pupils that their needs cannot be neglected, "nor can we expect in the near future that all pupils will be able to complete the secondary school as full-time students." Inglis estimates, conservatively, that more than a million children were leaving school above grade six, and he goes on to state: "Compared with this the number of those completing the secondary school course . . . is insignificant." One of the most compelling arguments for the junior high school (grades seven to nine inclusive), as presented by Inglis, was the need for giving those who left before entering grade nine some of the educational experiences hitherto reserved for high school youth.[5]

The establishment of junior high schools with at least the beginnings of a high school curriculum was one answer to the problem presented by the numbers who were leaving school after reaching age fourteen. But Professor Inglis, and presumably the other educators in his company, wanted to do far more than cope with the existing situation. And here we meet the reforming zeal of the educator and recognize it as one, but only one, of the factors in the process which transformed the high school. The NEA Commission, arguing that secondary education was essential for *all* youth, made the following specific recommendation: *"Consequently this Commission holds that education should be so reorganized that every normal boy and girl will be encouraged to remain in school to the age of 18 on full time if possible, other wise on part time."*

There are two points of interest about this recommendation. First, it appears inconsistent with one set of arguments in favor of the junior high school — the arguments based on the large proportion of pupils leaving school after reaching age fourteen. Second, it envisages part-time education as an alternative to full-time education. As to the first point, I think it clear that the writers of the Report feared that the raising of the school-leaving age would be a long slow process, and consequently it would be many decades before a large proportion of the sixteen- and seventeen-year-olds would be going to school. And they might well have been right, if the social and economic forces had been different. Actually, the raising of the school-leaving age in many states followed the change in the pattern of school attendance of a majority of the youth.

The second point requires a more lengthy comment. The possibility of part-time education by means of continuation schools was clearly very much in Professor Inglis' mind. He writes of the continuation school "so neglected in American education" and pleads that it be "given its legitimate and necessary place in coordination with the junior and senior high schools." The Commission is quite specific about the need for such schools, and in a recommendation which is rarely remembered nowadays, the authors express themselves as follows: "*Consequently, this commission recommends the enactment of legislation whereby all young persons up to the age of 18, whether employed or not, shall be required to attend the secondary school not less than eight hours in each week that the schools are in session.*"

The Commission admits in the next paragraph that it may be impracticable at the outset "to require such part-time attendance beyond the age of sixteen or seventeen," but maintains that eventually the period must be extended to eighteen. Furthermore, the Commission states that to make the "part-time schooling effective" it must be adapted to the needs of the pupils. And in order to develop "a sense of common interest and social solidarity" with those who are full-time students, the instruction should be given in the comprehensive high school rather than in separate continuation schools which "is the custom in less democratic societies."

This last is clearly a reference to Germany. And what is envisaged for the United States in this section of the Report is only a modification of the German practice of that day which, by the way, is still in operation. In Germany, then as now, part-time education begins at fourteen and is completed at sixteen; the formal instruction is given in special continuation schools. The Commission hoped that in the United States part-time education would be continued till age eighteen and provided in the same school which was accommodating those who desired full-time education through grade twelve. In other words, the comprehensive high school would enroll part-time as well as full-time students. Neither Professor Inglis nor the Commission prophesied as to what fraction of the youth would be enrolled part time and what fraction full time.

Let us see what actually happened in one large heavily industrialized state, New York. In 1919, the legislature enacted a law which required attendance of employed youth over fourteen and up to eighteen years of age in continuation schools for at least four hours a week during the day for thirty-six weeks and further required the establishment of such schools in districts of more than 5,000 in population. The law provided for the gradual development of a continuation school system to be started in September 1920 and to reach full capacity by September 1925. Contrary to the recommendation of the NEA Commission, the part-time students were cared for in separate schools of which fifteen were eventually established in New York City alone. The number registered in the continuation schools of the entire state rose steadily from 30,236 in 1921 to a peak of 168,377 in 1928; of these 131,022 were enrolled in New York City continuation schools. At this time, something like twenty percent of the age group fourteen to seventeen in New York State were enrolled in a continuation school for part-time education. During the same period (1921 to 1928), full-time enrollment in grades nine to twelve was also rising rapidly; some 270,000 more pupils were enrolled at the end of the period than at the beginning. (In these eight years, the population, age fourteen to seventeen, increased only by about 95,000.) In short, by 1928 about half the youth of New York were in school full time; about twenty percent in school on a part-time basis.[6]

I cannot help speculating about what would have been the course of American secondary education if the Depression had not occurred or had taken place a decade later. The pattern of secondary education had been transformed before

97

the Depression; this fact is perfectly clear. When it came to a choice between part-time and full-time school attendance, many youth preferred the latter. It would be a great error to assume that, even in New York State, anything closely resembling the German pattern of vocational education had been established. Furthermore, I am told that vocational as well as academic work was offered in the separate continuation schools set up in the larger cities of New York. There is no evidence that the employment opportunities were of the apprentice type supported by industry, as would be the case in Germany.

But the part-time enrollment fell during the Depression years, first slowly and then rapidly — from a peak of 168,000 in 1928 to 105,000 in 1933 and to about 30,000 just before World War II.[7] At first sight this swift decline in numbers would seem to show that the Great Depression had killed the continuation schools in New York. Yet a closer examination of the facts reveals that what actually happened was a transformation of the separate continuation schools into separate full-time vocational schools. The evidence in the case of New York is clear. Presumably, the situation was not very different in the other states which, in the 1920's, had also established continuation schools. In New York, the 1919 law had provided that, while employed youth were required to study only four hours a week, unemployed boys and girls had to study a minimum of twenty. Therefore, as employment opportunities declined, more and more young people were forced by law to lengthen their school attendance to at least twenty hours a week. As a matter of fact, many elected to do more and became essentially full-time students. In New York City, the school authorities, recognizing what had happened, officially converted the separate continuation schools into separate vocational schools, which became a firmly established part of the educational structure. These schools maintain a part-time continuation unit in which a few students are enrolled even at the present time.

The short-lived experiment of continuation schools on a large scale was a purely American attempt to answer questions that are still with us. How can you satisfy the youth who have little academic ability and whose interests lie in the direction of getting a job and developing a manual skill? How can you at the same time provide a general academic education for this type of student through twelve grades (or at least eleven) and at the same time prevent boredom and frustration? The continuation day school was one answer, though only four hours of formal instruction a week hardly satisfies our present idea of the amount of time which should be devoted to general education.

Another answer was in process of formulation just at the time the NEA Commission reported. This answer was to keep all youth in high school full time through grade twelve and provide the facilities and instruction for meaningful vocational education. And to forward this solution, the United States Congress passed the Smith-Hughes Act in 1917, appropriating money for vocational education. In his book, Professor Inglis indicated that he had great expectations for vocational education with the passage of the Smith-Hughes Act. (He was writing in 1917, remember.) It is clear that he and the members of the NEA Commission favored the development of vocational education within the comprehensive high school instead of in separate vocational schools. And such a development did take place in the next twenty years in many localities in many states. In three states — Massachusetts, Connecticut, and Wisconsin — the state authorities concerned with vocational education were unwilling to trust the principals of the general high school;

it was thought that the schools would be so academic in their orientation as not to give the vocational courses a fair chance. It was argued that only in separate vocational high schools could the federal and state funds be used to advantage for the education of boys in the skills of trade and industry. In New York City, as I have already pointed out, the fifteen continuation schools turned into vocational schools in the 1930's. A similar pattern seems to have developed in other large cities throughout the country.

I do not propose to enter into a discussion of the advantages and disadvantages of the separate vocational school. There are only a few cities where the issue now arises. What I should like to point out is how in the 1920's two rival methods of handling one educational problem were developed with the blessing of the professional educators and how the Depression essentially destroyed one method — the continuation school — and thereby favored the other — vocational education at the secondary level.[8] Of course, the two rival methods were different in their pedagogic content. Under the continuation school plan the learning of a skilled trade did not take place in school and only took place at all if suitable employment opportunity existed. The other method involved the student's devoting half his time in school in grades eleven and twelve to vocational work.

The victory of vocational education at the secondary level left unsolved the problem of the very slow readers. Quite rightly, vocational directors today refuse to have the educational facilities under their direction used as dumping grounds for those of very low academic ability. Under the continuation school plan, these students would have been better cared for, provided suitable employment was available and provided the required schooling occupied at least one-half the school day — two large provisos, I must admit.

Yet I see signs of a movement in the direction of some such scheme. I talked to a principal not long ago who arranged to have students experiencing great difficulty with their formal studies (in part because of lack of interest) come to school only in the mornings; in the afternoons they had a part-time job which was satisfactory.[9] What had been worked out in this particular school for a few students was quite similar to the type of part-time education envisaged by the NEA Commission in 1918; for, you will recall, the Commission recommended that the continuation classes be part of a comprehensive high school and *not* be offered in separate schools. Continuation schools and continuation classes still exist in some states and some cities but play a very minor role in the entire educational process. The amazing popularity of the continuation schools in New York in the 1920's has been almost entirely forgotten. There is no possibility of reverting to this type of education for any large numbers. I cannot help wondering, however, whether for certain kinds of pupils part-time education may not be the answer, assuming that suitable employment opportunites are available and that the boy or girl is sixteen years of age or older.

Let me summarize this chapter. For purposes of exposition, I have broken the revolutionary transformation of the high school which occurred between 1905 and 1930 into two parts. By so doing, I was able to see how the transformation looked to the reformers who were writing in 1918 at the midway point. Clearly, the total process is irreversible, though in two details — vocational education and the education of those who have great difficulty with their studies — the pattern is far from firm. To my mind, in these areas further searching examination is required. But for the examination to be profitable it must be city by city and town by town. I should start by questioning the dogma one often hears — that all the youth, irrespective of academic ability and interest, should complete grade twelve. Above all, the relation of education to employment of youth sixteen and over must be constantly kept in mind.

I have said the evidence is clear that we cannot turn the educational clock backwards; we cannot return to the situation of 1900 or even 1910. This is so because of complex social and economic changes in the United States which have created a society unlike any other in the world. Yet I do not want to close on what may appear to be an economic deterministic note. The reforming educators played their part in the whole transformation; to some degree they guided the boat, even if it was propelled by a power over which they had no control. Let me remind you of the reforming spirit which characterized the United States in the first two decades of this century. Education was believed in as though it were a newly discovered magic process. Presidents of colleges clinging to a classical pattern of education proclaimed its virtues as loudly as reformers like John Dewey. Such faith was in accord with the spirit of the day. American public opinion was predominantly in an optimistic humanitarian mood. One has only to remember the calls to political action of the elder LaFollette and Theodore Roosevelt to see why the radical transformation of the high school population was almost taken for granted by those who were American leaders just before World War I. Perhaps it would be fair to say that the changes in secondary education I have been discussing were the consequence of the harmonious reinforcement of a variety of forward moving currents in the history of this country — that the high schools of the 1930's (which followed essentially the same educational pattern as do high schools of today) were the creation of a prolonged surge of sentiment of the American people. I should call it a surge of noble sentiment. But my use of the adjective may only betray the fact that I was not only alive, but young, in the period when the waves of hope for humanity were running high.

I must confess, as I have reviewed the educational history of that period, I find my faith and optimism returning. So I venture to close this chapter with a prophecy. If the free world survives the perils that now confront it, I believe historians in the year 2059 will regard the American experiment in democracy as a great and successful adventure of the human race. Furthermore, as an essential part of this adventure — indeed, as the basic element in the twentieth century — they will praise the revolutionary transformation of America's treatment of its children and of its youth. They will regard the American high school, as it was perfected by the end of the twentieth century, not only as one of the finest products of democracy, but as a continuing insurance for the preservation of the vitality of a society of free men.

Appendices

Appendix A

KHRUSHCHEV'S MEMORANDUM OF
SEPTEMBER 21, 1958

This translation appeared in *The Current Digest of the Soviet Press*, October 29, 1958. It is reprinted here, as is Appendix B, with permission of *The Current Digest of the Soviet Press*, published weekly at Columbia University by the Joint Committee on Slavic Studies appointed by the Social Science Research Council and American Council of Learned Societies.

KHRUSHCHEV'S MEMORANDUM ON SCHOOL
REORGANIZATION

In Presidium of Party Central Committee: ON STRENGTHENING TIES BETWEEN SCHOOL AND LIFE AND ON FURTHER DEVELOPING A SYSTEM OF PUBLIC EDUCATION IN THE COUNTRY – The Proposals Set Forth in a Memorandum by Comrade N. S. Khrushchev, Published Below, Have Been Approved by the Presidium of the Party Central Committee. (Pravda and Izvestia, Sept. 21, pp. 2–3. Complete text:) Our system of education in the secondary and higher schools is now evoking a great deal of discussion. Many critical comments that reflect the true state of affairs are being made on this score.

Talks that I have had with secretaries of the Union-republic Communist Party Central Committees, with secretaries of territory and province Party committees and with other comrades who are thinking about questions of public education or are directly concerned with it and, finally, numerous talks with citizens have revealed serious dissatisfaction with the present state of affairs in the secondary and the higher schools.

The upbringing [vospitaniye] of the growing generation, which is called upon to erect the majestic edifice of communist society, is a matter of prime importance. The role of education is particularly great in our time, when it is impossible to develop the country's national economy successfully without making the broadest possible use of the latest achievements of science and modern technology.

In my speech to the 13th Congress of the Young Communist League, I already stated certain views on this vitally important question. I believe it would be useful to set forth in greater detail fundamental views on improving our entire system of public education in the country.

There is no doubt that in the 40 years of Soviet rule secondary and higher education in the Soviet Union has achieved considerable successes. While only 9,600,000 persons were enrolled in elementary and secondary schools in prerevolutionary Russia — in 1914 — enrollment at our general schools reached 28,700,000 in the 1957–1958 school year and, if one includes the adult schools, 30,600,000. In this time the number of students in the senior grades of secondary schools has increased almost fortyfold. Particularly great successes in public education have been achieved in a number of Union republics, the population of which was almost totally illiterate in the past. In the Uzbek Republic, for example, school enrollment now exceeds 1,300,000 whereas in 1914 there were barely more than 17,000 school children in the territory of what is now Uzbekistan.

The successes achieved in higher and specialized secondary education are also considerable. Only 182,000 students were enrolled in higher educational institutions and technicums in prerevolutionary Russia; today this number exceeds 4,000,-

ooo. Our higher schools have produced remarkable cadres of Soviet intelligentsia — engineers, agronomists, zootechnicians, teachers, doctors and other specialists. Today some 6,800,-ooo specialists with a higher or specialized secondary education are employed in the Soviet Union. Our successes in all branches of the national economy and the outstanding achievements of Soviet scientists, engineers and technicians, whose work has enriched the Soviet homeland and all mankind with discoveries of world significance, are largely due to the fact that the Soviet higher schools have been able to train skilled personnel capable of tackling the most complex and responsible tasks.

Nevertheless, we cannot be satisfied with the organization and very system of higher and secondary education. There are major shortcomings in the work of our schools and higher educational institutions, and these must no longer be tolerated.

The chief and fundamental defect of our secondary and higher schools is the fact that they are detached from life. Workers in public education and the higher schools have been criticized for this shortcoming many times, but to all intents and purposes the situation is almost unchanged.

The Secondary School. — Our general schools suffer from the fact that we have adopted many aspects of the prerevolutionary gymnasiums, the purpose of which was to give their students enough abstract knowledge to receive a diploma. At that time the state and the school were not interested in what happened to the graduates after they left school.

What is the goal of a secondary school when it prepares a person for a diploma? It is to impart a certain amount of academic knowledge that is not related to production. Until recently we had a certain shortage of young people with a completed secondary education. In the early years of Soviet rule, when the need arose to fill the higher educational institutions with workers, peasants and their children, and also with the children of office workers, scientists and representatives of the working people, the secondary schools in effect adapted themselves to preparing these people for admission to higher educational institutions. Since the secondary schools could not quickly cope with this task and, most important, were unable to supply higher educational institutions with trained people already connected with production from among workers and peasants, the Soviet government took the course of setting up workers' faculties, which enrolled adult workers, gave them a secondary school education and sent them on to higher educational institutions.

Gradually, however, the need for these faculties disappeared, and they have long ceased to exist. Also, the secondary schools no longer have the function of merely training young people for admission to higher educational institutions. Our country has set and is carrying out the task of giving young people a general secondary education. We try to put all our young people, millions of boys and girls, through the ten-year secondary school. Naturally not all of them can be absorbed by the higher educational institutions and specialized secondary schools. Hence it would be absurd to set as a goal that all young men and women who have received a secondary education must go to a higher educational institution.

But at present our ten-year schools are not accomplishing the task of preparing young people for life but are preparing them solely for admission to higher educational institutions. Among young people who have finished secondary schools, and among families and teaching staffs there is the firm belief that this is the way it should be, that our secondary schools are designed to train people solely for the purpose of assuring an enrollment for higher educational institutions, so that they can then receive a higher education.

Life has shown long ago that this conception of the tasks of the secondary schools is incorrect. Even formerly a large number of boys and girls did not enter higher educational institutions upon finishing secondary schools. And in recent years, because of the growing number of young people finishing secondary schools, a smaller proportion of boys and girls has been entering higher schools. The greater part of them, after completing studies in a secondary school and receiving a diploma, prove to be unprepared for life and do not know what to do next.

In present conditions, the higher educational institutions can admit approximately 450,000 students a year, half of them in the day divisions. But the majority of young people who have completed ten years of schooling prove to be unprepared for practical life. In the period from 1954 to 1957 more than 2,500,000 secondary school graduates did not enroll in higher educational institutions. In 1957 alone more than 800,000 secondary school graduates did not enter higher schools or technicums.

Because the secondary school curriculum is detached from life, these boys and girls have absolutely no knowledge of production. And society does not know how to utilize these young and vigorous people to best advantage. Consequently, a large number of young people and parents are dissatisfied with this situation. And this process is not slowing down but intensifying with time. It seems to me that this state of affairs should cause us great concern.

This situation can hardly be considered correct, and many comrades with whom I had occasion to speak expressed doubt about the correctness of our present system of universal ten-year education.

It is evidently necessary, in educating and bringing up children in the schools, to prepare them psychologically from the very first grade for taking future part in socially useful work, in labor, in creating values necessary for the development of the socialist state. In our country there is still an essential difference between manual and mental labor, and out of the heritage of the past there remains a situation in which preference is given to that part of the youth that must be enrolled in higher educational institutions and not go into the factories or collective farms. As for the remainder, they "have not made the grade" and "have not shown ability." It is they who must go to work. This is fundamentally wrong and runs counter to our doctrine and our aspirations.

Boys and girls who have finished secondary school generally think that the only acceptable path in life for them is to continue their education in a higher or, at least, specialized secondary school. A number of those who complete ten-year schools reluctantly go to work at factories, plants, and collective and state farms, and some of them even consider this to be below their dignity.

This haughty and contemptuous attitude toward physical work is also to be found in families. If a boy or a girl does not study well, the parents and those around the child frighten him by saying that if he does not study well, if he fails to receive a gold or silver medal, he will not be able to get into a higher educational institution and will have to work at a factory as a common laborer. Physical work becomes something with which to scare children. I am not even mentioning that such views are insulting to the working people of a socialist society.

This situation, in which people are brought up in our society without a respect for manual labor and detached from life, is wrong and can no longer be tolerated. After all, in a socialist society labor should be evaluated in terms of its utility; it should be stimulated not only by remuneration but also — and this is most important — by the high respect of our Soviet public. Young people should constantly be impressed with the fact that what is most important for society is that by which society lives, i.e., productive labor, because only this labor creates material values. Work is a vital necessity for every Soviet man.

It must be said that the practice that has existed until recently of creating higher-school admission privileges for persons who finished school with a gold or silver medal has complicated the situation even more. The point is that some parents who wanted their children to receive medals brought great pressure to bear on the teachers.

Furthermore, there are considerable defects in the very practice of selecting young people for admission to higher educational institutions. Although there are competitive examinations for admission to higher schools, it must be admitted that frequently it is not enough to pass an examination to enter a higher educational institution. Here, too, the influence of parents is considerable. There is good reason why young people entering higher educational institutions quite frequently say that after they have won in the admission competition, the competition among the parents begins, and it is this that often settles the matter. This creates inequality in admission to higher and specialized secondary educational institutions.

How can all these shortcomings of our schools be eliminated?

The system of bringing up our growing generation in the schools must be decisively reorganized.

The most important thing here is to issue a slogan and make this slogan sacred for all children entering schools — that all children must prepare for useful work, for participation in the building of a communist society. And any work at a factory, collective farm, Machine and Tractor Station or Repair and Technical Station or in an office — any honest, useful work for society — is sacred work and necessary for every person who lives in and enjoys the benefits of society. Every person living in a communist society must contribute his share of labor to building and further developing this society. Preparing our growing generation for life, for useful work, inculcating in our young people a deep respect for the principles of socialist society — this must become the main task of our schools.

It is the duty of the schools to give people a rounded education, to give them a good basic knowledge and at the same time prepare them to do systematic physical work, instill in young people a desire to be useful to society, to take an active part in producing the values society needs.

What practical measures would it be advisable to take in this direction?

In my opinion, all students without exception should be drawn into socially useful work at enterprises, collective farms, etc., after completing the seventh or eighth grades. In the cities, villages, and workers' settlements all school graduates should go to work; no one should skip this. In the first place, this will be democratic since equal conditions will be created for citizens: Neither the parents' status nor their pleas will exempt anyone from productive labor. Secondly, this will be a fine school for bringing up all young people in the heroic traditions of the working class and the collective farm peasantry.

Thus, the only possible condition for eliminating the shortcomings of our schools, an indispensable condition, is to train all boys and girls, while in school, for participation in physical work at plants, factories and collective and state farms, in any work that benefits society.

The entire system of our secondary and higher education should be so organized as to assure good training of cadres — engineers, technicians, farm specialists, doctors and teachers and factory and agricultural workers — of all the cadres that our state needs. Things must be organized in such a way that the training of all our cadres is better and more skilled than it has been so far.

With this aim in view, it seems advisable to divide secondary education into two stages. The first stage should apparently be a compulsory seven- or eight-year school. Public education workers and many parents maintain that an eight-year period of schooling will make it possible to do a better job of giving school children the necessary general and polytechnical education. Apparently this is true, but it is advisable that each Union republic decide these questions separately in accord with its own conditions. Serious thought will also have to be given to the content of the curriculum and the organization of studies at such a school.

In the eight-year school, the first stage of secondary education, attention should be focused on instruction in basic knowledge, polytechnical and labor training, the inculcation of communist ethics, the physical development of children and the fostering of good esthetic tastes in them. Here one must not overburden school children to an extent that is harmful to their health.

One must also not forget the specific features of women's labor. In our country men and women receive equal remuneration for the same quantity and quality of work. Nevertheless, because of specific everyday conditions, the woman has many other obligations, quite inevitable ones: She must know how to care for a child, keep house and do a certain amount of cooking. Public catering will develop even more extensively in the future, but apparently even in public catering the work of women will be predominant. Therefore, while in school girls must be taught cooking, sewing and dressmaking, and other women's occupations. The school curriculums should provide for all this.

It is necessary considerably to improve the material facilities of schools, to do away, at long last, with shifts and to provide schools with modern educational equipment.

The second stage of secondary education might take several directions. One might be, for example: After seven or eight years of instruction, the schools might stress special vocational training for the next two or three years.

In cities, factory centers and workers' settlements the children, after seven or eight years of schooling, should perhaps enter schools of the factory-training type. Here they would continue their studies, but these studies would be closely linked with vocational training and help the students to acquire production knowledge and labor skills; not only abstract knowledge of production, but labor skills too.

In rural areas the students, after seven or eight years of schooling, should obtain practical and theoretical knowledge in agronomy, zootechnology and other branches of agriculture or study a trade for two or three years, since in the countryside, too, young people can learn definite trades.

Thus, after finishing school, boys and girls will have both a proper education and production skills and will enter life well prepared.

But the following course is also possible: The first stage of secondary education could be completed in the eight-year schools, after which all the boys and girls would go to work. If the general schools are organized in this way, in the near future we will have to place 2,000,000 to 3,500,000 young people in jobs annually, about forty percent in the cities and the rest in the countryside.

The task of placing such a large number of young people is no simple matter, particularly since managers are now very reluctant to hire young people under 18. But this is a task of paramount Party and state importance. It will be necessary to break down the bureaucratic barriers impeding the placement of young people in jobs in the national economy and to instruct the U.S.S.R. State Planning Committee to draw up a long-range plan for the job placement of young people finishing eight-year schools. This plan should take into account the specific conditions of each administrative economic region, so that the young people will be given employment where they live.

Here, evidently, it is necessary to consider reserving jobs for young people at enterprises so that they may go right to work without difficulty after completing the eight-year school and consider setting up special shops at enterprises and assigning jobs suitable to the age and capacities of the young people, with strict observance of labor safety regulations.

Young people going to work upon completing the compulsory school (with an eight-year period of instruction) should be given the opportunity to learn a trade in various ways. One such way might be to teach a boy or girl a trade directly in production, primarily through the organization of short courses and brigade apprenticeship. Another way might be vocational training in a specialized one- or two-year vocational school. The question of the period of schooling, the curriculum and the organization of training in such a school should be thoroughly considered and discussed.

It may be found advisable to give only a part, rather than all, of the young people finishing the compulsory eight-year schools (those who will want it and will comply with the necessary requirements) definite vocational training in factory apprenticeship schools or in similar agricultural schools, mentioned above, in which the students, besides learning a trade, would study general disciplines. Until recently we had such schools, and they fully justified themselves. The factory-apprenticeship [FZU] and factory-training [FZO] schools, set up on the basis of seven-year schooling, that is, admitting girls and boys who had completed seven-year schools, turned out hundreds of thousands of people who, thanks to instruction in these schools, became skilled workers with a secondary education. A large number of graduates of these schools worked in production two or three years, then went on to higher educational institutions and, having successfully finished them, are now working as engineers in our industry, transport and construction.

In the rural areas the broad network of eight-year schools could be used for vocational training of young people by organizing twelve-month or six-month courses at them in which the eight-year school graduates could learn a mass agricultural trade of their own choice. Such courses could also be set up directly at large state farms, M.T.S. and R.T.S.

As a second stage, which would complete the secondary education, the training of boys and girls while they work would seem to be the most advisable. We should evidently have evening (shift) schools for working youth at enterprises. All boys and girls who go to work at a plant will be able, if they so wish, to obtain an education in such a school. It will probably be necessary to have a well-thought-out system of correspondence courses, in which training should be organized on a high level: lectures and the necessary study aids would be published and the necessary consultation made regularly available for those who want it.

It is necessary to prevent a situation in which the evening

schools make it their task merely to prepare young people for admission to higher educational institutions, since many more young people will attend these schools than the higher schools will be able to absorb. Consequently, these schools must give students the opportunity not only to receive a complete general secondary education but also to improve and broaden their vocational training, so that better-qualified and better-educated men and women workers, men and women collective farmers and other workers for our society are turned out with a complete secondary as well as specialized education.

Consequently, we will continue to give everyone the opportunity of obtaining a secondary education of the same scope as the curriculum of the ten-year school now provides — but not through the present ten-year school, which is detached from life, but through evening or correspondence courses, which we must develop and improve in every way. It may happen that a boy or girl, upon finishing school, will not feel a need for further study: He or she may grow tired or may not yet realize the necessity of having a secondary education. For a certain time this boy or girl will not study, but will work. These young people will have a certain lapse in their studies, but when they have entered life and become aware of the need to supplement their education, they will always be able to study, to obtain a secondary and, later, a higher education.

Thus, every boy and girl will be able, if he or she wishes, to receive a complete secondary education in evening educational institutions while working at factories and plants, participating in labor, not necessarily manual labor but perhaps working in an office, at any rate living by useful work in society. Such a system of upbringing will help young people to avoid becoming detached from life, so that boys and girls will enter life well prepared, as full-fledged workers of a communist society, by their labor taking a direct part in the creation of the material values that this society needs. It is necessary even in the schools to begin preparing people for production, for useful work in society. Give them as much education as possible and then send them into production. Working in production and studying in school, a young person will more easily find his place in society and determine his proclivities and desires. He can specialize in a given field and, after working for a while, enter an appropriate educational institution. But before this he should be tested in evening studies while working. I repeat that there must be no exceptions in this matter, regardless of the parents' status in society or the posts they hold.

Long before the proletarian revolution V. I. Lenin pointed out that the upbringing of young people under socialism could be correctly organized only if education were combined with the productive labor of the growing generation. "In order to link universal productive labor with universal education," wrote V. I. Lenin, "it is evidently necessary to obligate *everyone* to participate in productive labor" (Vol. II, p. 441, V. I. Lenin's emphasis).

Since the 20th Party Congress, work training has been introduced in our schools beginning with the junior grades; in the fifth to seventh grades the children spend two hours a week in school workshops, and in the senior eighth to tenth grades they have two hours a week of practice training in farming and machine shops and electrical work and 60 to 80 hours a year of production practice directly at enterprises and collective farms. This is undoubtedly a good thing, but it is still far from a combination of education and productive work; rather is it a general acquaintance of the students with various types of work done by adults.

K. Marx also pointed out that at a certain age children should work in production every day, and this is quite right, since only then can boy and girls understand the full complexity and joys of work and really become a part of a working collective and its interests.

In working out the specific regulations on reorganization of our schools, thought must be given to granting certain privileges to students of schools for working and rural youth who successfully combine studies and work in production. Perhaps they should be exempted from work two or three days a week so that they can devote this time wholly to their studies.

As for the period of instruction in these schools, it should probably be three or four years so as to prevent overburdening of the students. This question also requires special study.

I would like to emphasize once again that the proposals set forth in my memorandum on changing the system of schooling are not at all aimed at reducing the amount of secondary education and replacing it by seven- or eight-year schooling. Extensive development of the network of evening and correspondence schools will enable all those who wish it to receive a full secondary and, subsequently, higher education.

We must not forget that at present, despite the fact that seven-year education is compulsory, a large number of young people are not only failing to receive a full secondary education but are not even completing seven grades. According to figures of the U.S.S.R. Central Statistical Administration, in recent years only about 80% of the children who have entered the first grade have finished the seventh grade, even taking into account the pupils remaining in the same grade for a second year. This means that we have far from fully carried out the principle of compulsory seven-year education.

In my opinion, the above proposals on changing the system of public education will facilitate implementation of the principle of compulsory education in a seven- or eight-year school.

As for introducing universal compulsory full secondary education in the form followed in our country so far, this, according to all information at hand, would not be advisable at present.

The question arises: Should we change over completely to the proposed system of public education or would it be advisable to retain to a certain degree the present secondary school, making the necessary changes in its work? There is the view that a relatively small number of full secondary polytechnical schools might be retained, but with the condition that the amount of labor training and participation in productive labor be increased in them, and that the graduates of these schools be required to work a period of two years upon entering higher educational institutions. This question also requires careful and thorough discussion, after which the best solution must be found.

The new system of public education should provide, as an exception, appropriate secondary schools for particularly gifted children who at an early age clearly show an ability in, say, mathematics, music or the graphic arts. These schools would give these children the secondary education necessary for further study at an appropriate higher educational institution. Such schools are necessary so that our state can correctly develop and utilize the people's talents.

If reorganization of the schools is recognized as necessary — and life persistently demands it — this work must be done in such a way that no gap is created in training the necessary contingents for higher educational institutions. Matters must be so organized that in the period of transition from the present system of education to the new system no harm is done in the training of specialists for our national economy in the country's specialized secondary and higher educational institutions.

In this period of transition (three or four years) a certain number of existing ten-year schools should evidently be retained. Perhaps it will be found practical to select from among capable pupils at existing schools the particularly gifted children who show a bent for physics, mathematics, biology, drawing, etc., and to place them in particular schools. They should be better prepared for entry into higher educational institutions in accord with their aptitudes. Then our specialized higher schools will get young men and women who are better prepared to master the exact and other sciences.

The Higher School. — It is advisable to examine the system of higher education as carefully as that of secondary education. At present, many young people who finish higher education institutions have a poor knowledge of the practical side of things and are inadequately prepared for work in production.

Today boys and girls finish the ten-year school at the age of 17 and immediately enter an institute graduating from it at the age of 22 or 23. What kind of specialist do we get here?

One must also not forget how our young people now choose a vocation when entering a higher educational institution immediately after finishing school. In many, and perhaps even in most, cases this is a random choice. Hence it often happens that when a young person fails to get into a higher educational institution that he has chosen, he is ready to apply at any other higher school, even one with an entirely different specialization, just to obtain a higher education. There are also many instances where young specialists who have just finished a higher educational institution have no inclination to work in their chosen field and either enter another higher school or work in another field. This is primarily due to the fact that upon finishing school today young people have no experience in life.

The training of specialists in a number of fields is conducted incorrectly in the higher educational institutions too.

Let us take agriculture. In many capitalist countries students in higher agricultural schools must work on farms during their course of study. We, on the other hand, often bring up our students incorrectly. Take the Timiryazev Academy of Agriculture. There the students are trained not in the fields but primarily on small gardens. Cows and other animals are studied not on the farms, as life requires, but chiefly from models. For every student at the academy there is more than one person serving these students. And this is called a higher Soviet school! I consider this to be wrong.

Therefore I very often hear collective farm personnel say — and sometimes I even have to come to the defense of young specialists — 'We don't need young specialists, why do you send us young people?' I have heard such statements made at many collective farm meetings the moment the question of specialists was raised. And why? Because for the most part these young people are inexperienced. A young girl or boy comes to a collective farm: He or she fumbles about and essentially cannot help the collective farm chairman to improve the farm. It turns out that an untrained practical worker, a collective farm chairman or brigade leader, is more valuable to the farm than this newcomer, who, although theoretically well trained, does not know how to apply theory to practice. But if this young specialist had finished the educational institution perhaps three or four years later and gone through all the agricultural production processes himself, he would be of much more use. Then young specialists finishing our higher educational institutions would be regarded differently.

One might reply that even today our higher educational institutions require production practice. True, they do, but it is very poorly organized. Production practice should be conducted more thoroughly, not as it is now. Today students in work practice spend more time loafing at the factory; one works while 10 to 15 look on, themselves afraid to come near the machine. And the managers of enterprises place little trust in the students, since the latter have no qualifications and if they are given an operating machine there is a loss of production capacity and of production possibilities. Such students are a burden to the enterprises.

We must have students who know their trade to perfection. Then such students will be wanted in work practice, since they will have not only the necessary professional, vocational and labor skills but also a higher level of development and will be able to work more productively and show the workers how to perform an operation better and more efficiently.

Lastly, we must not ignore the fact that there are still few children of workers and collective farmers in the higher educational institutions. In Moscow higher schools, for example, children of workers and collective farmers comprise only 30% to 40% of the enrollment. The rest of the students are children of office employees and of the intelligentsia. This situation is clearly abnormal, of course, not to mention the fact that the number of workers and collective farmers themselves who are full-time students in our higher educational institutions is literally insignificant.

It is necessary to reorganize the system of higher education, to bring it closer to production and really link it with production. The higher educational institutions should admit young people who already have some experience and a record of practical work. Reorganization of the secondary schools will help us to find the proper solution to this question. The higher educational institutions should admit those who display greater ability and the desire to continue their schooling. Here it is necessary to consider not only the desire of the candidate for admission to a higher school but also the appraisal of his work by public organizations (trade union and Young Communist League), so that selection depends on the applicant's preparation, on his proclivities and on the assurance that the individual selected will justify the expenditures made on him and can really be a useful production leader.

In developing our higher schools, particularly the technical schools, the primary emphasis should be on evening and correspondence education. It seems advisable that in most higher educational institutions the first two or three years of study be combined with work. This will make it possible to select from among the enormous number of young people who will want to study those who show that this is not a passing fancy, that they really have a thirst for knowledge and are patient and industrious. Only after this, from the third year, can privileges be granted, such as exempting a student three days a week from work in production. In the last two years of study in higher educational institutions it may possibly be found advisable to exempt the students entirely from work in production, except for the time required for production practice.

In general the question of evening and correspondence higher and specialized secondary education must be carefully considered. We must make it possible for people who perform useful work for society to have a greater opportunity during their off-hours to attend, if they so desire, educational institutions where they could study the arts, painting, music, the humanities, etc. The state and especially the trade unions should assist the working people of our society in this matter.

In my opinion we should consider reviving the college-factories. These produced quite good results in the past; the national economy employs many engineers who received their training and diplomas in this way. It must be said that the overwhelming majority of them are very good engineers and specialists well versed in their fields.

In the higher agricultural schools we should probably combine education and agricultural work on a seasonal basis. Instruction should be given at institutes attached to big farms, to state farms. These should have school buildings, laboratories and a farm for field work. Or, at any rate, a higher agricultural school should have a large model training farm. The students themselves should care for the animals, repair the machines and know how to operate them and should themselves sow, cultivate and harvest crops.

The work of universities and of medical, pedagogical and other higher schools should also be closely linked with practice. The forms of these ties should be carefully thought out, of course.

There are many other shortcomings in the work of our schools: The students are excessively burdened with obligatory classes and have little time for independent study, and the teachers, among whom are many highly qualified specialists, take very little part in research. Instruction in the social sciences and the organization of ideological upbringing work require considerable improvement. Reorganization of the system of higher education should help to eliminate these shortcomings also.

The system of specialized secondary education should also be reorganized in these respects.

* * *

There are some ideas on secondary and higher education which I would like to add to what was already said at the 13th Y.C.L. Congress and which met fairly wide and favorable response in the country.

Perhaps it will be considered necessary to discuss these questions at a plenary session of the Central Committee, since they concern millions of people, all of society, and correct solution of them will be of great importance for the further material and spiritual development of our society.

After a discussion of this question at a plenary session, perhaps it will be found useful to work out appropriate theses for a nationwide discussion of these problems and then to convene a session of the U.S.S.R. Supreme Soviet to discuss problems of public education in the country and to determine the general line for their solution. This must be done in such a way, however, that specific resolutions on the secondary and higher schools are adopted in final form at sessions of the Union-republic Supreme Soviets, since a decision on the question of public education in each republic falls within the competence of the Union-republic Supreme Soviet.

One thing must be firmly stressed: An improvement of the entire matter of public education in the country is persistently dictated by life. — N. KHRUSHCHEV.

Appendix B

EXTRACT FROM THE DECEMBER 1958 LAW OF THE SUPREME SOVIET ON SCHOOL REORGANIZATION

The following extract is from a translation that appeared in *The Current Digest of the Soviet Press*, March 4, 1959.

LAW ON STRENGTHENING TIES BETWEEN SCHOOL AND LIFE AND ON FURTHER DEVELOPING THE PUBLIC EDUCATION SYSTEM IN THE U.S.S.R. (Pravda and Izvestia, Dec. 25, pp. 1–2.) The U.S.S.R. Supreme Soviet notes that the question of strengthening the ties between school and life and further developing the country's public education system submitted by the Party Central Committee and the U.S.S.R. Council of Ministers to the U.S.S.R. Supreme Soviet for consideration is of exceptional importance for successfully carrying out the task of building communism.

The nationwide discussion of this question has shown that the program drawn up by the Party Central Committee and the U.S.S.R. Council of Ministers for further developing the public education system has met with the unanimous approval and support of the working people.

[Then follow many paragraphs essentially repeating the arguments in Khrushchev's memorandum.]

The Supreme Soviet of the Union of Soviet Socialist Republics *resolves:*

To approve the theses of the C.P.S.U. Central Committee

129

and U.S.S.R. Council of Ministers "On Strengthening Ties Between School and Life and on Further Developing the Country's System of Public Education," which received universal support in a nationwide discussion;

To recognize the necessity of preparing children from their very first years in school for the fact that they must take part in socially useful work when they are older. From the age of 15 or 16 all young people must undertake to perform socially useful labor consonant with their ability, and the entire subsequent education of young people must be linked with productive labor in the national economy.

I. ON THE SECONDARY SCHOOL

Art. 1. The main task of the Soviet school is to prepare pupils for life and for socially useful labor, to further raise the level of general and polytechnical education, to prepare educated people well grounded in the fundamentals of science, and to bring up young people in the spirit of profound respect for the principles of socialist society, in the spirit of the ideas of communism.

A close tie between schooling and labor, between schooling and the practice of building communism, should become the guiding principle of instruction and upbringing in the secondary school.

Art. 2. Universal compulsory eight-year education shall be introduced in the U.S.S.R. to replace universal compulsory seven-year education.

The eight-year school is an incomplete general-education labor polytechnical secondary school which is to give pupils a firm grounding in general and polytechnical subjects, instill in them a love of labor and a readiness for socially useful activity and effect the moral, physical and esthetic upbringing of the children.

Educational and upbringing work in the eight-year school should be based on the combined study of the fundamentals of science, polytechnical training and labor upbringing and on the extensive enlistment of school children in forms of socially useful labor suitable to their age.

Art. 3. It is hereby established that a complete secondary education for young people, beginning at the age of 15–16, shall be provided on the basis of a combination of schooling and productive labor, so that all young people in this age group shall be enlisted in socially useful labor.

Art. 4. The following basic types of schools providing a complete secondary education are established:

a) schools for working and rural youth — evening (shift) general-education secondary schools, in which persons who have graduated from the eight-year school and are working in one of the branches of the national economy will receive a secondary education and raise their vocational qualifications. The term of study at these schools shall be three years.

To create the necessary conditions for students in evening (shift) general-education secondary schools, the U.S.S.R. Council of Ministers shall establish a shorter working day or a shorter working week for persons successfully pursuing a program of studies without taking time out from production;

b) general-education labor polytechnical secondary schools providing production training, in which persons who have graduated from the eight-year school will in a period of three years obtain a secondary education and vocational training for work in one of the branches of the national economy or culture.

The ratio between theory and practice in production training and the alternation of periods of instruction and work shall be determined in conformity with the nature of the specialized training and with local conditions. In rural schools the school year must be arranged with due consideration for the seasonal nature of agricultural work.

Production training and socially useful work may be conducted in training and production shops of nearby enterprises, in apprenticeship brigades of collective and state farms, at training-and-experimental farms, and in school and interschool training-and-production workshops;

c) technicums and other specialized secondary schools in which persons who have graduated from the eight-year school obtain a general secondary education and a specialized secondary education.

Art. 5. To enhance the role of society and to help the family in the bringing up of children, the network of boarding schools, extended-day schools and extended-day groups shall be expanded. It is hereby established that the boarding schools shall be organized along the lines of the eight-year school or general-education labor polytechnical secondary school providing production training.

Art. 6. Serious improvements are deemed necessary in the organization of upbringing work in the schools, so that the schools will instill in students a love for learning and labor and a respect for the working people, and will mold a communist world view in them and bring them up in the spirit of utter devotion to the homeland and the people, in the spirit of proletarian internationalism. One of the basic tasks of teachers, parents and public organizations is to further improve the work of training pupils in the habits of cultured behavior at school, within the family and on the streets.

Art. 7. It shall be considered essential to transform the existing ten-year schools (the senior grades) into urban and rural general-education secondary schools of various types.

The reorganization of the public education system shall be carried out in a planned and organized manner, with maximum consideration for local features, in no case permitting any deterioration in the schooling available to the population. Attention shall be directed to the need for further increasing the number of female students in indigenous nationalities in the upper grades of schools in the Union republics and autonomous republics of the [Soviet] East.

The plan to shift to the new school system must be worked out in each Union republic in conformity with its economic and cultural development. The shift from seven-year to eight-year compulsory education and the organization of various types of complete secondary schools must commence with the 1959–1960 school year and be completed in three to five years. Pupils now in grades eight through ten shall be assured the opportunity to finish secondary school according to existing study plans and programs, but with intensified labor training.

In planning for the secondary school reorganization, provision must be made to assure that an adequate number of secondary school graduates enter higher educational institutions, since there must be no interruption in the flow of young, highly skilled specialists into the economy. To this end a certain number of the existing secondary schools should be retained, if need be, in each Union republic during the transitional period.

Art. 8. The statutes on the compulsory eight-year school, the evening (shift) general-education secondary school and the general-education labor polytechnic secondary school providing production training shall be confirmed by the Union-republic Councils of Ministers.

Art. 9. The opening and closing dates and the vacation

schedule of the eight-year and general-education secondary schools are to be established by legislation of the Union republics.

Art. 10. The U.S.S.R. Council of Ministers and the Union-republic Councils of Ministers shall take measures to strengthen the material base of the schools, abolish multi-shift classes and organize production training, as well as measures to arrange facilities for vocational training and production practice for students in the upper grades of secondary school.

Art. 11. The Union-republic Councils of Ministers will take measures to provide refresher training for teachers and to staff the schools with teachers who have the necessary education to meet the new tasks facing the general schools, as well as measures to further improve the working and living conditions of teachers and raise their theoretical and ideological level.

II. ON TECHNICAL VOCATIONAL EDUCATION

Art. 12. The prospects for Soviet technical and economic development are making increasingly high demands on the production skills of workers in all branches of the economy. In these conditions the widespread development of technical vocational education for youth becomes particularly important.

The basic task of technical vocational education is the planned and organized training of cultured and technically-educated skilled workers of industry and agriculture for all branches of the economy, the communist upbringing of school children, their ideological tempering and the inculcation in them of a communist attitude toward work.

Art. 13. Urban and rural technical vocational schools [uchilishcha] shall be organized for the technical vocational instruction of young people who take jobs in production after completing the eight-year school.

Technical vocational schools shall be specialized according to branches of production and shall conduct their educational and upbringing work on the basis of the active and systematic participation of young people in production work and on the basis of close ties with enterprises, construction projects, state farms and collective farms.

Art. 14. Factory-plant training schools, trade schools, railroad, mining and construction schools, labor reserves farm mechanization schools, technical vocational schools, factory-plant apprenticeship schools and other vocational training institutions under the jurisdiction of the economic councils and agencies shall be reorganized into day or evening urban technical vocational schools with terms of one to three years or rural technical vocational schools with terms of one to two years.

The reorganization of existing vocational educational institutions into urban or rural technical vocational schools is to be accomplished in three to five years, with consideration for the individual features of the economic regions.

Art. 15. So that the technical vocational schools can gradually become partially self-supporting, the U.S.S.R. Council of Ministers and the Union-republic Councils of Ministers shall work out and consistently implement measures to expand and increase income from the production activities of educational institutions.

In connection with the increased material security of the working people, it is deemed advisable to change the existing level of material security provided the students by introducing the payment of apprenticeship wages instead of by providing free clothing and food, so as to heighten the student's interest in better mastering his chosen vocation.

Full state support shall be maintained for school children who are orphans, inmates of children's homes or children from large families.

Art. 16. Ministries, agencies, economic councils, enterprises, institutions and organizations shall provide the technical vocational schools with production equipment for training workshops and assure paying jobs at enterprises for the production training of students and also shall create conditions in which young people can pursue their program of studies successfully and master new machinery, advanced technology and efficient work methods.

Art. 17. The U.S.S.R. Council of Ministers and the Union-republic Councils of Ministers shall draw up long-range and annual plans for the vocational training of young people completing the eight-year general schools, technical vocational schools and secondary schools providing production training and plans for employing these young people, having in mind the establishment of a reserve quota of jobs for young people at enterprises and the strict observance of safety rules and regulations.

Art. 18. The reorganization of the system of technical vocational education means new and higher requirements regarding the level of technical, ideological, political and pedagogical training of production training specialists and teachers for technical vocational schools. The expansion of the network of these schools will increase the demand for specialists and teachers. Therefore greater attention must be devoted to the training of such personnel in technicums and higher educational institutions.

The quality of textbooks and visual aids must be improved and output increased, the production of technical educational and popular science films must be expanded, and radio and television must be widely utilized in technical vocational education.

Art. 19. The statutes on the technical vocational schools shall be confirmed by the U.S.S.R. Council of Ministers.

Art. 20. The U.S.S.R. Council of Ministers and the Union-republic Councils of Ministers shall work out measures to bring about fundamental improvements in the training of workers through individual, brigade or classroom instruction and to raise the qualifications of workers engaged in production.

III. ON SPECIALIZED SECONDARY EDUCATION

Art. 21. In industrial and agricultural production as well as in institutions of culture, education and health, an important role is played by technicians, who are the immediate organizers of production, and by other workers with a specialized secondary education.

The interests of modern production, which is based on the latest scientific and technical achievements, demand that graduates of technicums have a high level of theoretical training and a good knowledge of practice.

Therefore it is deemed essential that the system of specialized secondary education be further improved and that the training of specialists with secondary school qualifications be improved on the basis of a close tie between schooling and socially useful labor and of an extensive development of evening and correspondence education.

Art. 22. The training of specialists in specialized secondary schools shall be carried out on the foundation of the eight-year school and, according to individual specialties, on the basis of a complete secondary education.

The total amount of schooling and the length of specific periods of schooling with or without time out from production may vary, depending on the branch of the national economy for which the specialists are being trained and on the working conditions at enterprises, construction projects or other organizations.

Art. 23. It is hereby established that instruction in the specialized secondary schools must assure the students a secondary-school level general education as well as the necessary theoretical and practical training in their specialty, and in the technical and agricultural specialized secondary schools the students must also receive a qualification with a job rating in a worker's trade.

Art. 24. It shall be considered advisable to organize shops and workshops at industrial technicums in which the students will themselves produce goods and to organize large farms at agricultural technicums in which the students themselves will do all the basic work.

Art. 25. The network of specialized secondary schools shall be further expanded in the direction of bringing these schools closer to production — with consideration for the personnel needs of the economic regions — by implementing broad cooperation among the economic councils, ministries and agencies in the training of specialists with a secondary education.

The expansion and improvement of correspondence and evening education, as the basic form for the training of specialists with a specialized secondary education, shall be achieved by strengthening the correspondence and evening technicums and by organizing correspondence and evening divisions at full-time educational institutions which have qualified teachers and the necessary instruction and material base.

Persons working in occupations related to their chosen specialty shall be given priority of admission to evening and correspondence schools.

Art. 26. The statutes on specialized secondary schools shall be approved by the U.S.S.R. Council of Ministers.

IV. ON THE HIGHER SCHOOL

Art. 27. The tasks of communist construction demand that the higher educational institutions be brought closer to life and to production and that the theoretical level of specialist training be raised in keeping with the latest achievements of science and technology.

The further development and improvement of the system of higher education in our country must ensure better practical and theoretical training of specialists, a marked improvement in the communist upbringing of young people and the active participation of all teachers in bringing up students.

The chief tasks of the higher school are:

to train highly qualified specialists brought up on the basis of Marxist-Leninist teachings who have a high mastery of the latest achievements of domestic and foreign science and technology and a good working knowledge of their specialty and are capable not only of making the fullest use of modern techniques but also of creating the techniques of the future;

to carry out scientific research contributing to the fulfillment of the tasks of communist construction;

to train scientific and pedagogical personnel;

to raise the qualifications of specialists working in various branches of the economy, culture and education;

to disseminate scientific and political knowledge among the working people.

[Then follow articles 28 through 41 dealing with the organization of higher education.]

Art. 42. The reorganization of higher and specialized secondary education shall be completed in three to five years. beginning with the 1959–1960 school year. with consideration for national and local peculiarities, and shall be carried out in such a way that the number of specialists graduating yearly to work in the economy, in science and in culture steadily increases in conformity with the growing demand for such specialists.

* * *

The Union-republic Councils of Ministers shall submit to the Union-republic Supreme Soviets proposals, stemming from this law, which will ensure that the ties between the school and life are strengthened, that universal compulsory eight-year education is instituted and that general secondary, technical vocational, specialized secondary and higher education in the republics is expanded.

The U.S.S.R. Supreme Soviet considers that bringing the schools closer to life will create the necessary conditions for the better rearing of the growing generations, which will live and work under communism. The reorganization of the public education system will be of enormous importance to the further material and spiritual development of Soviet society, will enhance the role of the Soviet school in the education and upbringing of young people, will better assure the training of highly qualified personnel for all branches of the national economy, science and culture and will contribute in even greater measure to the growing might of the Soviet Union.

K. VOROSHILOV, Chairman of the Presidium.

U.S.S.R. Supreme Soviet.

M. GEORGADZE, Secretary of the Presidium.
The Kremlin, Moscow, Dec. 24, 1958.

Notes

Notes

I. THE CHILD, THE PARENT, AND THE STATE

1. Matthew Arnold, *The Popular Education of France with Notices of that of Holland and Switzerland* (London: Longman, Green, Longman, and Roberts, 1861).

2. J. S. Mill, *On Liberty and Considerations on Representative Government* (Oxford: Basil Blackwell, 1948), p. 94–97.

3. Khrushchev's memorandum is presented in full in Appendix A. Extracts from the text of the law passed by the Supreme Soviet to implement Khrushchev's recommendations are given in Appendix B.

4. The present situation in the Soviet Union is such that one cannot speak dogmatically about the structure of Soviet education. As successful as the Soviets have been in their educational efforts, most descriptions and statistical accounts available in English concern the ten-year school and ignore the fact that the whole system is undergoing sweeping changes under the Khrushchev School Reform (see Appendices A and B).

In April and again in September of 1958, Khrushchev indicated the direction in which he wished Soviet education to move. The details of his proposals, as approved by the CPSU Central Committee and the USSR Council of Ministers, were spelled out in a lengthy document in November. These "theses" were then put into law by the Supreme Soviet on December 24, 1958. The law itself is much less specific than the November "theses" which appear in George S. Counts' *Khrushchev and the Central Committee Speak on Education* (University of Pittsburgh Press, 1959), where the forty-eight theses are analyzed by Professor Counts.

For studies of Soviet education up to the time of the reform proposals, see Alexander G. Korol, *Soviet Education for Science and Technology* (Cambridge: The Technology Press of the Massachusetts Institute of Technology, and New York: John Wiley and Sons, 1957); U.S. Office of Education, *Education in the U.S.S.R.* (Washington: Government Printing Office, 1957); George S. Counts, *The Challenge of Soviet Education* (New York: McGraw-Hill Book

143

Company, 1957); and Harry D. Gideonse, "European Education and American Self-Evaluation," *The Educational Record*, vol. 39, no. 3, July 1958. For an excellent but brief summary of Khrushchev's reform, see "The Khrushchev School Reform," by Albert Boiter, in *The Comparative Education Review*, vol. 2, no. 3, February 1959. In the same publication, see Henry Chauncey's article, "Some Comparative Checkpoints Between American and Soviet Secondary Education." Professor Counts has brought his earlier book up to date with "The Real Challenge of Soviet Education," *The Educational Forum*, vol. XXIII, March 1959, p. 26. Two paragraphs are particularly worth quoting.

"The real challenge of Soviet education, therefore, is not to be found in the realm of science and technology," writes Counts. "If that were all we had to fear, the situation would not be too alarming. We must, of course, 'strive in the shortest possible historical period to overtake and surpass' the Soviet Union in whatever fields of science and technology they may be leading at the present time. About this there must be no equivocation. But after we have succeeded here the great task of our education will remain: the rearing of a generation of citizens who will be able to rise to the moral and intellectual challenge of these fateful times.

"This means above all the raising of our sights relative to the entire educational undertaking. And this means that we must regard education far more seriously than ever before in our history. . . . This means further, and most particularly, the raising of the qualifications and the material and spiritual rewards of the teachers at all levels."

5. A description of the youth organizations in the Soviet Zone of Germany is given in Chapter 8 of *Totalitäre Erziehung* by M. G. Lange (Frankfurt am Main, 1954); children between eight and fourteen are recruited into the "Young Pioneers", youth over fourteen into the "Free German Youth" (FDJ). The Sovietization of the schools and universities in the Soviet Zone is discussed at length in this same volume and in a book entitled *Stürmt die Festung Wissenschaft* by Marianne and Egon Erwin Müller (Berlin-Dahlem: Colloquium Verlag, 1953). The authors sum up the situation as it then existed with the statement: "The universities of middle Germany [the Soviet Zone] thus have only the name in common with those of the Federal Republic."

In the last six years conditions have become worse from the standpoint of a Western observer. The Communist puppet regime (the government of the so-called German Democratic Republic) has attempted to make the schools and universities more effective instruments of a totalitarian state with the consequence that a steady stream of professors, engineers, doctors, and scientists have escaped from the Soviet Zone (through Berlin) and settled in free Germany. The situation in the universities as it existed in 1957 is described by a professor in a West German university who remains anonymous in an article in *Confluence* (vol. 6, 1957, p. 58) entitled "The University in East Germany." The quotations from his account which follow would apply as well today (1959) as two years ago.

"In the Soviet world, the number of young people to be educated in a university, and the number of students in the separate disciplines, does not depend on the number who are prepared, but on the master-plan of the moment [p. 59]. . . . The Communist state invests every area of life with the aura of politics and ideology. . . . The work of professors and students of biology, medicine, mathematics, and literature must all be carried on in accord with the scientific foundation of Marxism-Leninism-Stalinism. It is this tapeworm of *isms* that assumes the fundamental position taken elsewhere by logic and objectivity, neutrality and empiricism. Consequently, 'Soviet science' being the 'most progressive' science in the world, has become the compulsory foundation for all German studies. The Russian language is a compulsory subject for every student in the Soviet Zone [p. 60]."

An article in the official "scientific" journal of the Socialist Unity Party is an example of the frank recognition by the Communists of the nature of education in a "workers' and peasants' state." After making derisive comments about the Social Democrats in the Federal Republic who think they can teach about socialism in the schools in that part of Germany, the author writes as follows:

"Our schools [i.e., in the Soviet Zone] are a part of the revolutionary transformation of our social life since 1945. From the beginning, we made no pretence of neutrality but dedicated our schools to the truly democratic new order of whose realization they were an active part. Our education corresponds to the Marxist idea that the goals, content, and function of education are always determined by the conditions and necessities of the life of that society which the young people will later enter. Every idea is fought which speaks of an 'autonomous pedogogy' or conceives of education with goals and tasks which are independent of time and any particular society or focuses on the 'child as such,' because in reality such ideas only serve the interests of the ruling class in an exploiting society." (Horst Reichert, *Einheit, Zeitschrift für Theorie und Praxis des wissenschaftlichen Sozialismus*, vol. 12, no. 5, May 1957, p. 571.)

6. An agreement between the states of the Federal Republic for

"unification in the field of education" was signed by the Minister-Presidents of the separate states in Düsseldorf on February 17, 1955. A Permanent Conference of the Ministers of Education of the different states was established ten years ago and has a secretariat. Through this medium many details of school and university organization are made more uniform between the states that would otherwise be the case. (Alinder M. Lindergun, *Germany Revisited, Education in the Federal Republic*, U.S. Department of Health, Education, and Welfare Bulletin, no. 12, 1957, Washington: Government Printing Office.)

7. There are three types of pre-university schools in Germany today and essentially the same three types in both German-speaking and French-speaking Switzerland. Corresponding to the three types are three somewhat different state examinations which must be passed in order to obtain a certificate which admits to a university. (And the certificate admits the holder to any university in the nation and to any faculty within one of the universities.) In the classical language Gymnasium, the study of both Latin and Greek is compulsory; in the modern language Gymnasium, Latin and at least one modern language are studied; in the mathematics–natural science Gymnasium, the student studies neither Latin nor Greek but must study at least two modern foreign languages and carries the study of mathematics and science somewhat farther than in the other two types of schools.

Programs in the different types of German pre-university schools are given on p. 48 of a publication in 1953 of the Office of the U.S. High Commissioner for Germany (H. P. Pilgert, *The West German Educational System*). For those who study Latin and Greek, 27 percent of the time of a student is devoted to these subjects; 10 percent to a modern language (French or English); 12 percent to German — a total of 49 percent. For those who do not study Greek, Latin occupies 8 percent of the students' time; two modern languages, 18; and German, 13 — a total of 39 percent. Similar programs that I have seen in Swiss schools are even more heavily loaded with linguistic studies. Mathematics, science, and history each occupy about 10 percent of the students' time; drawing, music, gymnastics, the balance. The scientific course, in which there is no Latin, devotes more time to mathematics and science. This is also true in Switzerland.

A middle school in Germany currently enrolls about 10 percent of the age group. Entry is at age ten plus, and the program is complete at sixteen. In Switzerland, in a number of cantons similar schools enroll a much larger proportion of the age group. They are often called "secondary schools"; the age of entry may be the same as that of the first stage of a Gymnasium. The course is usually completed before the student reaches sixteen years of age. One foreign language, mathematics, history, and the native tongue constitute the essential subjects, as a rule. In order to provide more flexibility in the system and obviate some of the difficulties of the early selection for the Gymnasium, various possibilities of transfer to the pre-university courses are provided in certain cantons. The long course in Latin, however, is a stumbling block. Programs that have the long sequential courses necessary for mastery of a language make for rigidity. Postponing the age at which the study of these difficult sequential subjects begins, therefore, seems to some reformers the only way of introducing more flexibility into the educational system.

Mention should be made of a fourth type of certificate issued in some Swiss cantons on the basis of examinations parallel to the three which yield a university entrance certificate. This is the Commercial Maturity Certificate. It admits to the business schools in certain cantons and to the economics section of the law faculty of certain universities. The course preparing for this examination is of the same length as the other pre-university courses but is less difficult. In some cantonal schools students studying all four programs are in one school. But this is not the usual type of organization. Often the students studying the classical programs and those studying the scientific are in different school buildings. As in Germany, coeducation in the pre-university schools is the exception rather than the rule.

It may be a comfort to Americans wrestling with some of our school problems to learn that in both French-speaking and German-speaking Switzerland there is complaint that the schools do not teach the children to write their native language as they should. (And this complaint is directed to the pre-university schools with their selected group of students!)

Not more than 20 percent of an age group are selected, as a rule, for entry into all the pre-university schools taken together in a given area. The age at which selection is made varies from canton to canton in Switzerland and from state to state in the Federal Republic of Germany. There is a great difference of opinion on this subject in both countries among laymen and educators. If a nine-year course is regarded as essential (as it often is by the proponents of the classical curriculum), the pupil must enter at age ten, having completed only four years of the elementary school. In West Berlin, however, the separation is postponed several years, and the course in the pre-university schools is reduced to only five years. (See *Germany Revisited*, cited in note 6 above, p. 31 and 35.) In Switzerland the pre-university school course is seven to nine years, depending on the canton.

Whether the age of entry into the pre-university school is ten or later, a vital decision must be made — first by the parent, then by the school authorities. The standards of selection are usually high and may be based on an examination, or the opinion of the elementary school teachers, or the school record. Children of families with a long professional tradition may be rejected. Complaints are heard, but the system remains unaltered. (In several Swiss cantons I visited, where families with educational ambitions seemed to be making trouble for the authorities, careful explanations of the significance of the selection process were given to the parents of the ten-year-olds each year.) Even when the boy or girl has been admitted to the boys' or girls' pre-university school, the selective process is by no means over. A long hard road lies ahead before the completion of the seven- to nine-year course and the passing of the examination that yields a certificate admitting to any university in the country. A half or more of the pupils fail during the course and are dropped from the school; in one canton I visited in Switzerland, only a third of those who entered finally graduated. Those who succeed have acquired a general education which meets the European standard for an educated man or woman — a mastery of two foreign languages, mathematics through calculus, European history, and the literature of the nation. The students are then ready to enter a university. Only about 5 to 7 percent of an age group complete the course in one of the pre-university schools in Germany or Switzerland, and about the same percentage enter a university. In the United States, more than 30 percent of an age group enter a four-year institution of higher learning.

For those who are not selected or do not wish to be selected for enrollment in a pre-university school, full-time education will usually end with the completion of eight or nine years of elementary school work (age thirteen or fourteen). The vocational schools in Germany (*Berufschulen*) are continuation schools in that they are attended for six to eight hours each week. They are, nonetheless, of great importance. They are considered to provide the "book learning", such as practical mathematics and blueprint reading, necessary for those in various types of apprentice training; they are likewise regarded as important instruments for "educating students to being morally valuable members of society, filled with love for their professional (vocational) activities and conscious of their responsibility as citizens of a democratic state" (Hans Wenke, *Education in Western Germany*, Washington: Library of Congress Reference Department, European Affairs Division, 1953). Attendance at these schools is compulsory for two or three years after leaving the elementary school (*Volkschule*). The special technical school (*Fachschule* or *Technikum*) was developed in Germany at the beginning of this century. It is open to those who have completed several years of apprentice training and demonstrated ability to profit from the course. Several excellent schools of this type exist in Switzerland, and I have visited the one in Biel. In this school, at least, the mathematical studies and the scientific work were carried on at an advanced level, and I would hazard the opinion that in some fields the graduate would be as well educated as in many of our undergraduate engineering schools. The proportion of young men attending these schools is small. See J. L. Henderson, "Education in Modern Germany: An Appraisal," *Educational Forum*, vol. XXI, 1957, p. 316–326.

8. There has been some concern both in the Federal Republic of Germany and in Switzerland about the supply of scientists and engineers. Whether or not there are too many now attending the German universities may be an open question. One of the factors leading to the downfall of the Weimar Republic was probably the vast unemployment of university graduates in the early '30's which, in turn, reflected the larger enrollments in the universities in the '20's (Walter M. Kotschnig, *Unemployment in the Learned Professions*, Oxford; 1937, p. 117–121). With this phenomenon in mind, Germans are not likely to be impressed with arguments for expanding greatly the size of the universities. But an entirely separate question is the one raised by the obvious fact that much potential talent is lost because of the failure of some bright children even to try to enroll in a pre-university school.

One of the few things that the Communists have done in the Soviet Zone that some free Germans might admit was a step forward is the opening up of the universities to children of workers and peasants. The methods by which this has been accomplished are those of a totalitarian state and certainly cannot be copied, but the contrast is striking between the small fraction of working-class children in the universities in the Federal Republic and the very large fraction of the same type of students in the universities in the Soviet Zone. The anonymous author of the article on "The University in East Germany" (see note 5, above) describes the difficulty of the middle-class parent in placing a child in a university in the Soviet Zone and then goes on to say: (p. 62) "Thus there is no attempt in the Soviet Zone to fill what we recognized as the all too justified need for equality of opportunity and education. With regard to the individual cases, this practice is more unjust than the situation in the universities of Western Germany, where, as in the past, only four out of a hundred students come from laboring families. In the Federal Republic, all educational institutions are accessible to all; unfortunately what is lacking is a generous scholarship policy. In the Soviet Zone, sixty percent of the students have to be from 'worker and peasant' families." One high official of a German state in which the Social Democrats have held office almost continuously complained that, in spite of all that had been done to make secondary and higher education free and widely available, very few sons and daughters of peasants and workers had taken advantage of the opportunities offered.

9. *Pierce, Governor of Oregon et al. vs. Society of Sisters; and Pierce, Governor of Oregon et al. vs. Hill Military Academy* (268 U.S. 510–536) 1925.

The people of Oregon passed an initiative measure in 1922, effective in 1926, that would require children to attend a public school. A Catholic parochial school and an independent school obtained preliminary injunctions restraining officials from enforcing the law. The State of Oregon appealed the granting of the injunction. The Supreme Court gave its opinion in 1925.

The decision states that "no question is raised concerning the power of the State reasonably to regulate all schools, to inspect, supervise and examine them, their teachers and pupils; to require that all children of proper age attend some school, that teachers shall be of good moral character and patriotic disposition, that certain studies plainly essential to good citizenship must be taught, and that nothing be taught which is manifestly inimical to the public welfare." The court then proceeds to point out that "the inevitable practical result of enforcing the Act under consideration would be destruction of appellees' primary school. . . ." and that "these parties are engaged in a kind of undertaking not inherently harmful, but long regarded as useful and meritorious." Reference is made to an earlier case as follows:

"Under the doctrine of *Meyer v. Nebraska*, 262 U.S. 390, we think it entirely plain that the Act of 1922 unreasonably interferes with the liberty of parents and guardians to direct the upbringing and education of children under their control. As often heretofore pointed out, rights guaranteed by the Constitution may not be abridged by legislation which has no reasonable relation to some purpose within the competency of the State. The fundamental theory of liberty upon which all governments in this Union repose excludes any general power of the State to standardize its children by forcing them to accept instruction from public teachers only. The child is not the mere creature of the State: those who nurture him and direct his destiny have the right, coupled with the high duty, to recognize and prepare him for additional obligations."

The case of *Meyer v. State of Nebraska* concerned a law passed by the state legislature in 1919 which made it a misdemeanor to teach any language other than English before a pupil had passed the eighth grade. The supreme court of the state had upheld this law, but, in an appeal to the Supreme Court of the United States under the Fourteenth Amendment, the decision of the state court was reversed. The opinion of the United States Supreme Court in part was as follows:

"Plaintiff in error taught this language [German] in school as part of his occupation. His right and the right of parents to engage him so to instruct their children, we think, are within the liberty of the Amendment [the Fourteenth]. . . .

"For the welfare of his ideal commonwealth, Plato suggested a law which should provide: 'That the wives of our guardians are to be common, and their children are to be common, and no parent is to know his own child, nor any child his parent. . . . The proper officers will take the offspring of the good parents to the pen or fold, and there they will deposit them with certain nurses who dwell in a separate quarter; but the offspring of the inferior, or of the better when they chance to be deformed, will be put away in some mysterious unknown place, as they should be.'

"In order to submerge the individual and develop ideal citizens, Sparta assembled the males at seven into barracks and intrusted their subsequent education and training to official guardians. Although such measures have been deliberately approved by men of great genius, their ideas touching the relation between individual and state were wholly different from those upon which our institutions rest; and it will hardly be affirmed that any legislature could impose such restrictions upon the people of a state without doing violence to both letter and spirit of the Constitution."

Private schools, of course, are subject to control by the state. Compulsory attendance laws require attendance in a *satisfactory* school (see note 10). As in so many other matters, the amount and nature of the control exercised by the state over private schools varies greatly from state to state. Perhaps it would be fair to say that, in general, some state control exists, but it is less than in the case of the tax-supported schools. In New York State, for example, courses of study beyond the first eight grades must provide for instruction in such matters as the English language, civics, hygiene, physical education, and American history, in addition to the other subjects mandated by the legislature for the public schools. The Regents' regulations in regard to graduation requirements do not apply to private schools.

10. In the last few years South Carolina, Mississippi, and Virginia have repealed their compulsory attendance laws. See the *Southern School News* of April 1955, March 1956, and February 1959. For other states see *Compulsory School Attendance and Minimal Educational Requirements in the United States*, by Ward W. Keesecker, revised by Alfred C. Allen (Washington: U.S. Department of Health, Education, and Welfare, Office of Education, Circular No. 440, March 1955).

The number of high school graduates in 1955-56, as a percentage of eighth-grade enrollment in 1951-52, varied from a high of 93 percent in Wisconsin to a low of 43 percent in Mississippi, with a median among all the states of 64.7 percent. These figures illustrate once again the impossibility of generalizing about American education.

The doctrine that each of the sovereign states had the responsibility to provide free elementary schooling was widely accepted by the third quarter of the nineteenth century. (For an account of the struggle over this issue see R. F. Butts and L. A. Cremin, *A History of Education in American Culture*, New York: Henry Holt and Company, 1953, p. 202-206.) Compulsory education for children (as apart from youth) had been established as early as 1642 in the Massachusetts Bay Colony (see Butts and Cremin, p. 102-108). For the subsequent battle over compulsory education see Butts and Cremin, p. 102-108 and p. 415-416. Butts and Cremin state that "by 1900 thirty-two states, embracing most of the North and West, had passed such laws, and with Mississippi's acceptance of the principle in 1918 the idea became universal." The Supreme Court of the United States in 1885 *(Barbier v. Connolly*, 113 U.S. 27-37), referring to an issue raised under the Fourteenth Amendment, declared that: "the Fourteenth Amendment . . . undoubtedly intended not only that there should be no arbitrary deprivation of life or liberty . . . but that equal protection should be given to all under like circumstances. . . . But neither the Amendment — broad and comprehensive as it is — nor any other Amendment was designed to interfere with the power of the State, sometimes termed its police power, to prescribe regulations to promote the health, peace, morals, education and good order of the people. . . ." In a later decision the Supreme Court referred to education as "one of the purposes for which what is called the 'police power' may be exercised."

11. See *Compulsory Education Requirements* cited above in note 10. The complexity that exists among the states in regard to the whole matter of compulsory school attendance, work certificates and child labor laws, and part-time education is matched by the complexity within a single state. In New York, for example, there is a host of laws covering all these topics. Full-time attendance is required of all children between seven and sixteen; employment permits are required for all minors under eighteen, with certain exceptions; minimum ages are set for employment in various kinds of occupations; and provisions in the large cities for part-time or continuation schooling are made for minors between sixteen and seventeen who are out of school.

While students drop out before high school graduation in all states, not all states provide part-time schooling for young people who have left school. Exact information is very difficult to obtain, but it would appear that about half the states make provisions for these boys and girls. In some of these states part-time schooling is mandatory, whereas it is permissive in others. There is little question that continuation programs enroll a very small fraction of high school drop-outs. In Chapter IV, I make further mention of the problems involved with students who have little interest in school and leave as soon as they can.

12. Jefferson's ideas about education have been often referred to, particularly in the last thirty or forty years. In a letter to John Adams on October 28, 1813, after noting that the first session of the Virginia Legislature after the Declaration of Independence had abolished entail and primogeniture, he writes as follows: "These laws, drawn by myself, laid the axe to the foot of pseudo-aristocracy. And had another which I had prepared been adopted by the legislature, our work would have been complete. It was a bill for the more general diffusion of learning. This proposed to divide every county into wards of five or six miles square, like your township; to establish in each ward a free school for reading, writing, and common arithmetic; to provide for the annual selection of the best subjects from these schools, who might receive, at the public expense, a higher degree of education at a district school; and from these district schools to select a certain number of the most promising subjects, to be completed at an University, where all the useful sciences should be taught. Worth and genius would thus have been

sought out from every condition of life, and completely prepared by education for defeating the competition of wealth and birth for public trusts." (Saul K. Padover, *The Complete Jefferson*, New York: Duel, Sloan, and Pearce, Inc., 1943, p. 284-285.)

It is interesting to note that one of Jefferson's plans for educational reform (which did not materialize) calls for education as an instrument to prevent the growth of a "pseudo-aristocracy." In modern terms, we should say it was a plea for free schools and free higher education in order to insure a high degree of social mobility. Jefferson also often argued for universal education at the elementary school level. For example, in a letter to Colonel Yancey in 1816 he wrote: "If a nation expects to be ignorant and free, in a state of civilization, it expects what never was and never will be. . . . I know of no safe depository of the ultimate powers of the society but the people themselves; and if we think them not enlightened enough to exercise their control with a wholesome discretion, the remedy is not to take it from them, but to inform their discretion by education." (Saul K. Padover, editor, *Democracy, by Thomas Jefferson*, New York: D. Appleton-Century Company, 1939, p. 137-138.)

It was this latter argument that President Garfield put first in replying to Lord Macaulay's famous letter to a prominent American written in 1857. The British historian had predicted the eventual collapse of any nation which had universal suffrage. "It is quite plain," he wrote, "that your government will never be able to restrain a distressed and discontented majority, for with you the majority is the government, and has the rich who are always a minority absolutely at its mercy." In an address in 1873 on "The Future of Our Republic: Its Dangers and Its Hopes," Garfield spoke of Macaulay's letter and declared "that this opinion of Macaulay's is vulnerable on several grounds. It leaves out the great counter-balancing force of universal education." He then went on to contrast the British class system with what had developed in the United States and said: "We point to the fact that in this country there are no classes in the British sense of the word — no impossible barriers of caste." His second argument thus is based on his belief that the pseudo-aristocracy which Jefferson set out to destroy in Virginia at the time of the Revolution had, in fact, largely if not entirely disappeared in the United States.

In a publication of the Educational Policies Commission of the National Education Association in 1937, Jefferson's ideas as to the ends to be attained by education are summarized from his writings as follows:

"(1) To give to every citizen the information he needs for the transaction of his own business,

"(2) To enable him to calculate for himself, and to express and preserve his ideas, his contracts, and accounts, in writing;

"(3) To improve, by reading, his morals and faculties;

"(4) To understand his duties to his neighbors and country, and to discharge with competence the functions confided to him by either;

"(5) To know his rights; to exercise with order and justice those he retains; to choose with discretion the fiduciary of those he delegates; and to notice their conduct with diligence, with candor and judgment;

"(6) And, in general, to observe with intelligence and faithfulness all the social relations under which he shall be placed."

(*The Unique Function of Education in American Democracy*. The first draft was prepared by the historian Charles A. Beard.)

13. One often hears of local, state, and federal responsibilities in education, but there is still another level that is seldom mentioned. Between the state department of education in the capital of the state and the local district closest to the people there is an intermediate level of control in thirty-four states. These intermediate districts serve areas comprising two or more local districts which operate separately. As agents of the state departments of education, superintendents in these districts bring state supervision closer to the local level than would be the case were there no intermediary. These districts also provide additional services that each local district might not be able to provide for itself.

There are three kinds of intermediate districts. The county is by far the most common type. A second type is found in New York and the New England states, where the intermediate district is a supervisory union made up of a number of towns. The third type is the township, which continues to exist as an intermediate district in a few states — Michigan, Wisconsin, and Illinois, for example.

New Jersey is an example of a state in which the county is an intermediate district and in which the county superintendent's relationship to the state is clearly defined. He is appointed by the chief state school officer, and he is paid by the state treasury. Through him state aid to schools is apportioned and through him state educational policy is carried out. In Pennsylvania, on the other hand, county school administration is tied more directly to the local district level. Although his salary is paid by the state, the county superintendent is elected to office by a convention of members of all the local district school boards that do not employ a local superintendent. In addition, there is a county board of education which is also elected by the local board members. A last illustration of the diversity found among the states is Missouri, where the county superintendent is elected by the qualified voters of the county.

It should be noted that there are thirteen states in which the county serves *not* as an intermediate district, but as the local district, with a single school board and superintendent and no subordinate administrative organization. Large cities in these states often are independent districts. This county-unit system seems especially appropriate for rural areas. The county-unit states are Alabama, Florida, Georgia, Kentucky, Louisiana, Maryland, New Mexico, North Carolina, Tennessee, Utah, Virginia, West Virginia, and Nevada. Delaware has created special districts with no intermediate districts between them and the State Department of Public Instruction.

Much of the above material was taken from Shirley Cooper and Charles O. Fitzwater, *County School Administration* (New York: Harpers, 1953). See also The Department of Rural Education Yearbook, *The Community School and the Intermediate District* (Washington: National Education Association, 1954).

14. See Grace S. Wright, *High School Graduation Requirements Established by State Departments of Education* (Washington: U.S. Department of Health, Education, and Welfare, Office of Education, Circular No. 455, revised January 1958). The table on the next page shows the number of states requiring instruction in basic subject areas.

Accredited is the term used most often by state agencies to describe schools which meet various standards, among them graduation requirements. After an initial rating, subsequent accreditation is generally based on annual reports required in nearly all states. Some of the more common standards cover the length of class periods, school day, and school year; minimum number of teachers and preparation of teachers; libraries; school plant; pupil load, etc. For a summarization of various state practices and trends, see *State Accreditation of High Schools: Practices and Standards of State Agencies*, by Grace S. Wright (Washington: Government Printing Office, 1955).

One should note, also, the role of the six regional associations of colleges and secondary schools in the maintenance of standards — New England, Middle States, Southern, North Central, Northwest, and Western. Whereas state accreditation or approval may include every high school, the regional associations tend to be more selective.

Subject requirements of state departments of education — high school grades 9–12 [a]

Subject	Number of States											
	Number of Units										Other [b]	No requirement
	4	3½	3	2 or 3	2½	2	1½	1 or 2	1	½		
English	18	1	19								1	10
Social studies			9	1	3	17	4	9	1		2	3
Mathematics						2	1	1	27			18
Science						[e]5		2	25			17
Health and/or physical education	1					3	1	1	15		10	18
Fine or practical arts						1			4			44

[a] Includes ninth grade requirements for Minnesota, Pennsylvania, and Utah, although these states count only units earned in grades ten to twelve to compute graduation requirements. For purposes of simplification, a unit can be considered the equivalent of one year's work in a particular subject.

[b] Instruction is required but units of credit are not specified.

[c] In two states practical arts, and in one state a foreign language, may be substituted for one year of science.

In 1933 they instituted jointly a Cooperative Study of Secondary-School Standards, which resulted in four volumes, among them *Evaluative Criteria*, a lengthy and detailed checklist covering many aspects of school organization and program. Several states suggest the use of this document for self-evaluation.

Finally, one should note that in two states, California and Michigan, the state universities are the accrediting agencies, while the state departments of public instruction approve schools for state aid. There is no uniformity among the states in the use of the terms *accreditation* and *approval*. Part of the confusion stems from the fact that accrediting originated with the state universities and was tied to college preparation. Gradually, the state departments of education took over the accrediting function, and in many states the term took on a much wider meaning.

15. Though I am told that the New York Legislature has been wiser than some in not interfering directly with matters of curricu-

lum, even in New York absurdities can be found. Section 804 of the Education Law is worth quoting, for it illustrates what I believe to be the folly of legislatures' mixing into curriculum matters. I by no means wish to imply that I am not in sympathy with the objectives of Section 804; but I fail to see how this law could possibly be implemented effectively, and I wonder if there is a single school system in New York State which does so.

"Section 804. *Instruction regarding nature of alcoholic drinks.*

"1. The nature of alcoholic drinks and their effects on the human system shall be taught in connection with the various divisions of physiology and hygiene, as thoroughly as are other branches in all schools under state control, or supported wholly or in part by public money of the state, and also in all schools connected with reformatory institutions.

"2. All pupils in the above-mentioned schools below the second year of the high school and above the third year of school work computing from the beginning of the lowest primary, not kindergarten, year, or in corresponding classes of ungraded schools, shall be taught and shall study this subject every year with suitable textbooks in the hands of all pupils, for not less than three lessons a week for ten or more weeks, or the equivalent of the same in each year, and must pass satisfactory tests in this as in other studies before promotion to the next succeeding year's work, except that, where there are nine or more school years below the high school, the study may be omitted in all years above the eighth year and below the high school, by such pupils as have passed the required tests of the eighth year.

"3. In all schools above-mentioned, all pupils in the lowest three primary, not kindergarten, school years or in corresponding classes in ungraded schools shall each year be instructed in this subject orally for not less than two lessons a week for ten weeks, or the equivalent of the same in each year, by teachers using textbooks adapted for such oral instruction as a guide and standard, and such pupils must pass such tests in this as may be required in other studies before promotion to the next succeeding year's work. Nothing in this section shall be construed as prohibiting or requiring the teaching of this subject in kindergarten schools.

"4. The local school authorities shall provide needed facilities and definite time and place for this branch in the regular courses of study.

"5. The textbooks in the pupils' hands shall be graded to the capacities of fourth year, intermediate, grammar and high school pupils, or to corresponding classes in ungraded schools. For students below high school grade, such textbooks shall give at least one-fifth their space, and for students of high school grade, shall give not less than twenty pages to the nature and effects of alcoholic drinks. This subject must be treated in the textbooks in connection with the various divisions of physiology and hygiene. and pages on this subject in a separate chapter at the end of the books shall not be counted in determining the minimum. No textbook on physiology not conforming to this section shall be used in the public schools.

"6. All regents' examinations in physiology and hygiene shall include a due proportion of questions on the nature of alcoholic drinks and their effects on the human system.

"7. In all state teachers colleges and state colleges for teachers adequate time and attention shall be given to instruction in the best methods of teaching this branch, and no teacher shall be licensed who has not passed a satisfactory examination in the subject and the best methods of teaching it."

16. *The Concord Daily Monitor and New Hampshire Patriot,* February 19, 1959. New legislation has been proposed to meet the problem.

17. In Article V of the New York State Constitution, the Regents are given the power "to appoint and at pleasure remove a commissioner of education to be the chief administrative officer of the department." In *The State and Education: The Structure and Control of Education at the State Level* by Fred F. Beach and Robert F. Will (Washington: U.S. Department of Health, Education, and Welfare, Office of Education, 1955), it is pointed out that there is an increasing acceptance of a pattern in which a state board of education is considered a policy-making agency for the schools of the state and the chief state school officer is its professional executive officer. This is the picture in New York, where the Commissioner is appointed by and is responsible to the Regents. In 1945, only eight state boards of education had the power to appoint the chief state school officer; in 1954, eighteen states followed this pattern. Seven of the states made the change from a popularly elected commissioner or state superintendent, and three changed from a governor-appointed chief state school officer. In 1954, there were twenty-six states which used popular elections and four states which used the system of appointment by the governor. From 1949 to 1954, no states with a system of appointment by a state board changed their patterns.

The fact that in New York the legislature bestows upon the

Commissioner final judiciary authority in school matters is particularly important in assessing his power. This judicial authority has been in almost constant existence since 1822 and is clearly stated in the statutes under Section 310 of the Education Law. The Commissioner is "authorized and required . . . to examine and decide appeals to him by persons conceiving themselves aggrieved in consequence of any action by school trustees, district superintendents, and other school officers or authorities and other public officers in any matters pertaining to the State's school system." Further, "His decisions in such appeals, petitions, or proceedings shall be final and conclusive, and not subject to questions or review in any place or court whatever."

Until recently this vast power of the Commissioner has not been challenged. A bill was passed in the 1956 session of the legislature to provide for review of his decisions under Section 310 by the State Supreme Court. The Governor vetoed the bill, however.

18. Georgia Senate Bill No. 221 was subsequently defeated. See *Legislation and the Curriculum:* Consensus Statement of the Members of the National Citizens Council for Better Schools, October 1958, p. 6. The position taken by the National Citizens Council in regard to legislative action in curriculum matters is worth quoting. The consensus statement from the document mentioned follows. Of seventy-seven members voting, two expressed reservations but agreed to the conclusion.

"It is the consensus of the members of the National Citizens Council that Congress and the state legislatures have a most important role to play in the encouragement and support of school improvement. There are many appropriate ways in which official concern for better schools can be translated into effective action. It is our firm conviction, however, that legislatures should not attempt to control the specific courses of study in our local schools by legislative fiat.

"There are two particular areas of school affairs in which intense public interest may tempt legislative action today. The first of these is the science and mathematics curriculum. The second is the training and the needed supply of teachers in these subjects. We are convinced that teaching and learning in these subjects can be most effectively promoted by encouraging and supporting improved instruction and learning in all subjects. Science and mathematics should not be given preferential treatment that would throw the total school curriculum out of balance, nor should science and mathematics teachers be made into a specially privileged class within the teaching profession. Either action, we believe, would prove more harmful than helpful in the long run."

19. The Board of Education of Massachusetts was created by the state legislature in 1838, largely as a result of the efforts of James G. Carter, who had been urging for some years the appointment of such a board and the establishment of state teachers' colleges. Carter is sometimes referred to as the "father of the normal schools." He was appointed by the governor as a member of the first Board of Education, but, contrary to what many expected, he was not made the secretary. Horace Mann, a lawyer by profession and a member of the state legislature, became the first secretary. In this capacity he performed great services on behalf of public education. What he wrote about the training of teachers in his first report (1838) is of interest today, in view of the skepticism one meets in certain quarters as to the possibility of developing teaching skill through formal training. "No one can entertain a doubt," he wrote, "that there is a mastery in teaching as in every other art. Nor is it less obvious that within reasonable limits this skill and this mastery may themselves be made the subject of instruction and be communicated to others. We are not left to the deductions of reason on this subject. In those foreign countries where the greatest attention has been paid to the work of education, schools for teachers have performed an important function in their system and with the happiest result." In regard to the first public institutions for training teachers, Butts and Cremin point out (p. 287): "Considerable opposition to these institutions developed in the state legislature from groups who thought they were an attempt to 'Prussianize' the schools." It is not always realized that state-supported institutions for training teachers in the United States were first set up primarily as an imitation of a European practice. (For the present-day situation see the following note.)

20. In view of widespread public criticism of the certification practices among the states, it may be worth while to give some facts taken from *A Manual on Certification Requirements for School Personnel in the United States*, by W. Earl Armstrong and T. M. Stinnett (Washington: National Education Association, 1957 edition). First, however, it is well to point out that the development of certification laws was the result of a determined effort to raise the caliber of teachers in our public schools; it was not the result of some kind of diabolical plot as one sometimes hears these days. The fear in the past was that without certification standards un-

qualified personnel would enter teaching; now the fear seems to be that the proliferation of requirements acts as a deterrent to men and women who would be good teachers. Whether present certification laws actually serve their purpose of upholding quality is a question which must be studied state by state.

All states require instructional, administrative, supervisory, and special school personnel in public schools to possess a certificate issued by a designated state authority. Eleven states require private and parochial school teachers to hold certificates; a number of others require certification of teachers if a private school seeks accreditation by the state. In seven states the authority of the state department of education to issue certificates is shared with certain cities — New York City, Chicago, Baltimore, for example. Ten states require examinations for certification. In 1957, a total of thirty-seven states required the minimum of a bachelors degree for a regular elementary certificate (thirty-nine states in 1959); in the same year all states but one required the minimum of a bachelors degree for a regular high school certificate, and four states required five years of higher education. The number of kinds of certificates issued varies enormously — from two in Connecticut and Hawaii to sixty-five in New Jersey.

It is not true, as one sometimes hears, that it is impossible to obtain a teaching job without meeting all certification requirements. With the teacher shortage there has been widespread use of emergency certificates for people who have not met all requirements. In 1957, all of forty-seven states reporting, except for Kansas and Massachusetts, issued emergency certificates under certain conditions. At that time, some twenty-six states did not have any rigorous regulations regarding minimum preparation in subject matter or education courses for the issuance of these certificates. The Research Division of the NEA estimated in 1958–59 that one teacher in thirteen held an emergency certificate (95,721 of a total 1,291,929 classroom teachers).

For a regular certificate all states enforce certain general requirements which are usually mandated by law. These often include age, citizenship, evidence of good health, and license fees. About twelve states require special courses in the particular state's history. Such courses ordinarily require attendance at an institution within the state. Needless to say, this requirement has been under considerable attack recently.

More widespread is the criticism of the alleged discrepancy between the number of subject-matter and the number of education courses required. It is sometimes said, for example, that a prospective

English teacher does not take enough English courses because he has to take courses in methods of teaching, educational psychology, educational history, and philosophy. In the table on the next page, taken from the *Manual on Certification*, note that, except for chemistry and physics, the median requirement of semester hours in education courses (eighteen) is equaled or exceeded by the median requirement in the academic field. (A semester hour is defined as one hour a week of lecture or class instruction for one semester, or its credit equivalent of laboratory work, field work, or other types of instruction. A year's work, two semesters, consists generally of thirty to thirty-two semester credit hours. A four-year program thus means from 120 to 138 semester hours.) The reason for the lower requirements in chemistry and physics is that these subjects are within the broad field of science, and it is presumed that students will have other science credits. In general, and this fact is not revealed by this table, requirements in special fields like music, art, and agriculture are heavier than academic requirements.

One very practical reason for not requiring more semester hours of specialization in a teaching field is the existence of 17,000 senior high schools (out of a total of 21,000) which, in my opinion, are too small to do an adequate job. In these small schools, each teacher must teach not one subject, but many, and this fact means that specialization in preparation is not realistic. The physics teacher, for example, must teach biology and chemistry as well, and probably some mathematics if he is to have a full teaching load. I doubt that many teachers exist who can handle effectively all these areas. One of my strongest recommendations is the elimination of the small high school through consolidation. The efficient use of teachers with specialized knowledge is not possible otherwise. (See p. 36–39 for further discussion of the small school.)

I have not investigated this whole matter of teacher training except to gather some facts together. I have no opinion on what elementary teacher training should be, but I do have a tentative opinion on the training of high school teachers. As with the recommendations in my published Report (*The American High School Today*, New York: McGraw-Hill Book Company, 1959, hereafter referred to as my Report), this one is based on what I know will work. I refer to the Master of Arts in Teaching program which is in operation at several universities, Harvard among them. This is a five-year program which has as its fundamental premise the thought that prospective teachers should be certified in their subject-matter specialty by the faculty of arts and sciences and certified in education courses by the faculty of education. The master's degree which results

Semester hour requirements for high school teachers in professional education and academic fields and subjects in 1957

Subject	No. of States in calculation *	Range	Median	Average
(1)	(2)	(3)	(4)	(5)
Professional education	52	12–27	18	19—
English	49 (3 M)	12–48	24	24
Modern languages	49 (3 M)	12–48	20	22+
Mathematics	49 (3 M)	12–40	18	20—
Science	38 (3 M; 11 ROS)	12–48	24	25+
Physical science	29 (3 M; 20 ROS)	8–40	18	22+
Chemistry	28 (3 M; 21 ROS)	6–30	17	18
Physics	29 (3 M, 20 ROS)	5–30	16	17—
Biological sciences	33 (3 M; 16 ROS)	12–40	18	22—
Biology	26 (3 M; 23 ROS)	5–30	18	18
General science	39 (3 M, 10 ROS)	12–40	18	22+
Social science	46 (3 M; 3 ROS)	10–48	24	26+

Legend: M, requirement is completion of major. ROS, requirements otherwise specified.
 * Includes states with specific requirements. States specifying requirements under another category or requiring completion of majors are not included. Majors, because of variation, cannot be translated into semester hours. States for which requirement may be specified in another category, or for which requirements are not stated in certification prescriptions, should not be interpreted as having no requirements for teaching the field or subject.

is, therefore, a joint degree bestowed by two faculties. It is significant, I believe, that a committee on teacher training of the National Council of Independent Schools has endorsed the Master of Arts in Teaching degree. See *Preparation of Teachers for Secondary Schools* (Boston: National Council of Independent Schools, 1958), p. 25.

I am prepared to argue that *in general* a high school teacher should have studied both a subject-matter field with a considerable degree of concentration and also professional courses in education. However, it seems to me that some way should be found to make exceptions for a *few* who have been outstanding students in liberal arts colleges and who wish to teach and are ready to prepare themselves to pass examinations for certification by a course of reading. West Virginia has such a scheme. See Genevieve Starcher's "National Teacher Examinations: A Certification Instrument in West Virginia" (*The Journal of Teacher Education*, Volume X, Number 1, 1959).

21. See Arvid J. Burke, *Financing Public Schools in the United States* (New York: Harper and Brothers, 1958), Table 7, p. 249, and the table in note 22 below.

22. The following table is taken from the *Statistical Summary of State School Systems 1955-56*, Samuel Schloss and Carol Joy Hobson (Washington: U.S. Department of Health, Education, and Welfare, Office of Education, Circular No. 543), p. 7. See *Rankings of the States*, Research Report 1959-R4, of the Research Division of the National Education Association for 1957-58 figures.

School revenue receipts (taxes, appropriations, etc.) by source: 1955-56 [a]
(figures represent percentages of total revenue receipts)

Region and State	Federal	State	Intermediate	Local [b]
Continental U.S.				
1955–56	4.6	39.5	1.8	53.9
1953–54	4.5	37.4	3.1	54.7
Northeast	2.6	34.0	c	63.4
Connecticut	4.9	26.3	——	68.7
Maine	5.2	27.1	——	67.7
Massachusetts	3.5	21.2	——	75.2
New Hampshire	5.9	5.5	——	88.4
New Jersey	2.5	24.2	c	73.2
New York	2.0	35.7	——	62.3
Pennsylvania	2.2	46.0	——	51.8
Rhode Island	5.5	15.9	——	78.6
Vermont	4.9	25.7	——	68.5
North Central	3.6	30.9	2.8	62.4
Illinois	3.6	24.0	c	72.4
Indiana	2.7	33.5	.3	63.3
Iowa	2.8	13.2	1.0	81.5
Kansas	6.1	23.2	16.6	54.0
Michigan	2.6	48.5	.3	48.6
Minnesota	3.5	39.9	4.2	51.7
Missouri	4.9	36.5	6.7	51.7

School revenue receipts, by Source: 1955-56 (table continued)

Region and State	Federal	State	Intermediate	Local b
Nebraska	5.0	6.5	10.1	77.9
North Dakota	4.2	25.8	21.4	48.6
Ohio	3.8	30.0	c	66.2
South Dakota	6.0	10.1	16.6	67.3
Wisconsin	3.8	19.4	3.2	73.4
South	6.9	54.3	.8	37.6
Alabama	7.6	73.8	—	18.3
Arkansas	11.2	42.4	—	46.5
Delaware	3.0	83.7	—	13.3
Florida	5.3	53.2	—	41.5
Georgia	8.0	64.8	—	26.9
Kentucky	8.4	35.9	—	55.5
Louisiana	4.6	63.0	—	31.5
Maryland	8.3	32.6	—	58.7
Mississippi	7.7	51.9	12.2	28.2
North Carolina	6.1	69.0	—	23.2
Oklahoma	7.4	43.1	7.3	42.2
South Carolina	4.8	74.5	—	20.7
Tennessee	7.2	58.7	—	33.8
Texas	4.8	53.9	.3	40.5
Virginia	13.8	34.9	—	50.6
West Virginia	4.6	59.5	—	35.8
Dist. of Columbia	14.1	—	—	85.9
West	5.5	39.7	3.9	50.7
Arizona	7.9	30.9	10.8	50.2
California	4.6	41.1	2.1	52.0
Colorado	6.3	18.6	8.0	66.9
Idaho	5.9	25.6	13.7	54.9
Montana	5.8	24.8	27.7	41.7
Nevada	15.2	41.2	—	43.7
New Mexico	12.7	64.9	—	22.4
Oregon	3.6	26.4	3.6	66.4
Utah	5.7	37.8	—	56.3
Washington	7.0	53.7	4.6	34.6
Wyoming	3.4	39.5	4.9	50.5
Outlying Parts of United States				
Alaska	19.1	49.3	—	31.6
American Samoa	—	—	—	—
Canal Zone	100.0	—	—	—
Guam	—	—	—	100.0

School revenue receipts, by Source: 1955-56 (table continued)

Region and State	Federal	State	Intermediate	Local [b]
Hawaii	11.3	—	—	88.2
Puerto Rico	17.8	—	—	82.2
Virgin Islands	12.0	—	—	87.8

[a] Revenue receipts in the form of gifts, tuition, and transportation fees are not included and constitute over one percent in only three states — Iowa, North Carolina, and Wyoming.

[b] When a county operates public schools directly, it is classified here as "local"; but when a county serves as an administrative unit between the state and local school districts it is classified as "intermediate." See note 14 above.

[c] Less than 0.05 percent.

23. The Smith-Hughes Act of 1917 provided for the promotion of vocational education by a permanent appropriation of $7,138,331 annually. In 1924, 1931, and 1950 Congress extended appropriations to Hawaii, Puerto Rico, and the Virgin Islands. The George-Barden Act of 1946 is the major supplement to the Smigh-Hughes Act. It provided for the further development of vocational education and authorized an annual appropriation of $29,267,081. Funds are provided under these acts by the federal government on a matching basis to the states for programs in agricultural education, distributive education, home economics, and trade and industrial education. Title VIII of the National Defense Education Act of 1958 amends the George-Barden Act by authorizing Congress to appropriate to the states $15,000,000 for each of four years on a matching basis to assist in the training of skilled technicians in fields necessary for national defense.

See the *Digest of Annual Reports of State Boards for Vocational Education* (Washington: U.S. Department of Health, Education, and Welfare, Office of Education, Fiscal Year 1956) for a detailed breakdown of expenditures and vocational education enrollments. See also L. S. Hawkins, C. A. Prosser, J. C. Wright, *Development of Vocational Education* (Chicago: American Technical Society, 1951) for a history of vocational education and the text of the Smith-Hughes and George-Barden Acts referred to above.

A brief historical account of the role of the federal government in education up to 1929 is to be found in the volumes published by the National Advisory Committee on Education appointed by President Hoover in 1929. Part I, "Committee Findings and Recommendations," and Part II, "Basic Facts," were published in Washington, D.C., in 1931. Part II contains a large amount of statistical information and a summary of the Supreme Court decisions affecting public education. It is interesting that the Committee did not look with favor on either the use of matching grants of federal money to states or the amount of federal control involved in the Smith-Hughes Act. Among the recommendations of the committee of fifty-two citizens "engaged or interested in education" were the following:

"2. *Amend Laws.* Amend those existing laws which give or tend to give the Federal Government and its agencies power to interfere with the autonomy of the States in matters of education. These amendments should repeal all provisions that require the States and their local communities to match federal funds or that grant power to the federal agencies to approve or reject state educational plans, to prescribe the standards controlling instruction, or otherwise to supervise and direct educational or research activities within the States.

"The foregoing discussion does not relate to federal research activities in fields other than education save as these affect the autonomy of the States in the conduct of their educational affairs.

"3. *Restrict legislation.* Enact no additional laws that grant federal financial aid to the States in support of special types of education or that increase existing federal grants for such special purposes as are already aided."

These recommendations, like the others of the Committee (note 12 Chapter II) seem to have had little or no effect on what has actually happened. Today, the annual federal appropriations for vocational education are over thirty-three million dollars.

24. The National Defense Education Act of 1958 contains ten sections or titles and authorizes about one billion dollars in federal aid. Some important features are noted below.

Title I — General Provisions. Here are set forth Congressional findings and policy declarations, which include prohibition of federal control over the curriculum, administration, or personnel of any school system.

Title II — Student Loans. This title provides federal assistance in the establishment of low interest loans to students at institutions of higher learning. Up to one half of a loan to a student (no loan in the aggregate may exceed $5,000, or $1,000 in any one year) is cancelled if the student becomes a full-time teacher in a public elementary or secondary school. The cancellation proceeds at the rate of ten percent of the loan plus interest each academic year of service. I might note that many people have seriously questioned the fact that students receiving loans are required to sign loyalty oaths.

Title III — Programs for Science, Mathematics, and Modern Foreign Language Instruction. This title authorizes three related programs:

(a) matching grants to state agencies for projects of schools for the acquisition of laboratory or other special equipment for science, mathematics, or modern foreign language teaching in public elementary or secondary schools or junior colleges;

(b) loans to nonprofit, private elementary and secondary schools for the same type of projects;

(c) matching grants to state agencies for expansion or improvement of supervisory services in science, mathematics, and foreign languages.

Title IV — National Defense Fellowship. This program is to increase the number of students in graduate programs, especially students interested in teaching in colleges and universities.

Title V — Guidance, Counseling, and Testing; Identification and Encouragement of Able Students. Two related programs are authorized:

(a) matching grants to state agencies to assist them in establishing and maintaining programs of testing, guidance, and counseling in secondary schools;

(b) federal contracts with institutions of higher learning to provide institutes to train personnel in counseling.

Title VI — Modern Foreign Language Development. Two related programs are authorized·

(a) federal contracts with institutions of higher education for paying one half the costs of establishing and operating centers for teaching modern foreign languages (and related instructions necessary for an understanding of the countries involved);

(b) federal contracts with institutions of higher education for short-term or regular institutes for advanced training of persons engaged in, preparing for, teaching (or supervising or training teachers) of languages in elementary or secondary schools.

Title VII — Research and Experimentation in the Use of Various Visual-aid Material. Grants and contracts are authorized to public or nonprofit individuals or organizations for projects and experimentation in the use of such aids as television, radio, and motion pictures for educational purposes.

Title VIII — Area Vocational Education Program. Matching grants to the states are authorized for the training of skilled technicians.

Title IX — Science Information Service. The National Science Foundation will provide for a more effective dissemination of scientific information.

Title X — Improvement of Statistical Services of State Educational Agencies. Matching grants are authorized to the state to strengthen statistical services.

I think it is fair to say that the National Defense Education Act is in the tradition of the Smith-Hughes Act and is contrary to the spirit of the recommendations of the National Advisory Committee on Education appointed by President Hoover in 1929 (see note 23, above).

25. The Summer Institute Program of the National Science Foundation has grown rapidly since its inception in 1953. Its specific objective is to improve subject-matter mastery of the participating teachers during the six- to ten-week courses which take place at sponsoring colleges and universities. As I write, for the summer of 1959 approximately 2,000 college and 17,000 high school teachers (roughly one-eighth of the total high school science and mathematics teachers in the country) have been awarded stipends to participate in the program. The total cost of the 350 institutes will be about $22,000,000.

II. EDUCATION IN THE SECOND DECADE OF A DIVIDED WORLD

1. J. B. Conant, *Education in a Divided World* (Cambridge, Massachusetts: Harvard University Press, 1949). The subtitle, "The Function of the Public Schools in Our Unique Society," summarized my discussion of educational topics. The first two chapters ("America's Fitness to Survive" and "The World Divided") presented the international situation as I then envisaged it. A different and far more optimistic prognosis of the future had been presented earlier in *Education and the Peoples Peace* (Washington: Educational Policies Commission, 1943). Among the four assumptions about the future on which were based the proposals for an international educational effort was the following:

"This document assumes that the United Nations will remain united in victory. The nature of the bonds between them will change, to be sure, in the new situation. The purposes to be served by unity will not, however, be greatly different. These nations will remain united, we assume, because that will be the only way in which they can realize for their people the full fruits of the military victory."

American Education and International Tensions, published by the same Commission in June 1949, concludes with the statement that "the present circumstances of international tensions are likely to continue into the adulthood of children now in school. . . ." The concern of the profession in those days with the ideological implications of the cold war is evident throughout the document of 1949. The section in the summary dealing with "The Totalitarian Threat" is worth quoting in full as an illustration of what then seemed to many educators a major concern of the public schools:

"Knowledge of the cold war, the reasons why it must be successfully waged, and of the principles and issues at stake are important. Loyalty to American ideals must continue to be a major purpose of education. Such loyalty should include an understanding of the elements in our national tradition worthy of the greatest devotion, of the qualities in our national greatness most worthy to be admired and fostered, and of the historical background and reasonable aspirations of other peoples. Provincial unconcern about problems beyond our borders is not adequate to the needs of the present day.

"With the prospect of continuing ideological conflict, four main lines of strategy for American education are suggested:

"(a) Young citizens should have an opportunity to learn about the principles and practices of totalitarianism, including those represented by the Soviet Union and by the Communist Party in the United States.

"(b) Teaching about Communism or any other form of dictatorship does not mean advocacy of these doctrines. Such advocacy should not be permitted in American schools.

"(c) The schools should continue with vigor their programs for giving young citizens a clear understanding of the principles of the American way of life and a desire to make these principles prevail in their own lives and in the life of their country.

"(d) Members of the Communist Party of the United States should not be employed as teachers."

2. California is an example of a state where the publicly supported colleges and universities are coordinated into a reasonable system. The local two-year college serves both those who wish to terminate their education at the end of one or two years beyond high school and those who wish a four-year program. The University of California welcomes properly qualified candidates who have completed

two years in a local community college for admission to the junior year at Berkeley, Los Angeles, or the other university campuses. In many other states, no such tradition has as yet been established, and, in some, there is clearly a competition between the four-year institutions and the two-year institutions for state funds. One way of saving money in at least a few states would be to provide for a better coordination between the institutions competing for the tax-payer s dollar.

3. In a weekly magazine with a wide circulation, a writer stated in early 1958 that "the facts of the school crisis are all out in plain sight and pretty dreadful to look at. First of all, it has been shown that a surprisingly small percentage of high school students is study-ing what used to be considered basic subjects. Only 12.5% are taking 12th-grade mathematics, and only 25% are studying physics. A foreign language is being studied by fewer than 15% of the students." In an interview which appeared in another weekly magazine a year before Sputnik, a critic of the public schools said in effect that (a) a great many high schools don't offer courses in basic science, geometry, and algebra, and more than half of the high schools offer no physics; (b) at the turn of the century a far larger percentage of the high school students were studying science and mathematics than is the case today.

These statements are typical of many that have appeared in the daily press in the last few years. To my mind, the use of national statistics, either in praise or in condemnation of the public schools, completely misses the point and proves nothing. In the first place, such national figures include some 21,000 schools, many of which, given a normal distribution of academic ability, are too small to pro-vide the teachers necessary to teach courses like physics and chemistry except at exorbitant expense (see p. 36). The only validity of national statistics on schools failing to offer advanced courses is to point up the crucial need for school consolidation.

In the second place, the lumping together of all high school students into a national statistic is equally misleading. All students are not of equal ability, and the testimony of teachers, in addition to common sense, indicates the folly of expecting a dull child to study physics with profit. What one wants to know is the percentage of bright students who are taking these advanced subjects in par-ticular schools. This is a meaningful figure and can lead to con-structive action. See p. 70-71 for a discussion of the academic inven-tory.)

Finally, nothing at all is gained from comparing national statistics of today with those of sixty years ago. The composition of the student body has altered so drastically that such a comparison is utterly meaningless. (See Chapter IV, "The Revolutionary Transformation of the American High School," for a brief history of this revolution in the composition of the student body.)

4. At present there are about 21,000 senior high schools in the United States. About 4,000 of these are, to my mind, large enough (a graduating class of at least one hundred) to provide adequately for a student body with a normal distribution of academic ability. Two thirds of all high school seniors attend these 4,000 schools; the other third are scattered among 17,000 schools. This means that of the total 1,500,000 seniors, 500,000 are in small high schools which I think should be consolidated.

If consolidation were to reduce the number of seniors in small schools from 500,000 to 150,000, or from one third of all the seniors to one tenth, we would have at the most between 12,000 and 13,000 high schools. The 150,000 still in small high schools would be scattered among 5,100 schools (5,100 : 150,000 : : 17,000 : 500,000). The 350,000 seniors in newly consolidated schools with graduating classes of one hundred would be in 3,500 schools (350,000 ÷ 100). Finally, there would be the original 4,000 schools of sufficient size that already enroll 1,000,000 seniors. The total number of schools is, then, 12,600 (5,100 + 3,500 + 4,000). This figure, I think, is a realistic one to aim at. In my Report, I gave the figure 9,000 as the maximum number of schools needed, which would be true if all 500,000 seniors in small schools attended newly consolidated schools (500,000 ÷ 100 + 4,000). It seems clear, however, that some small schools must remain, though it is reasonable to assume they need not enroll more than ten percent of all high school students.

5. In areas where geography is, in fact, the obstacle to consolidation, there are various solutions, all of which cost money. The first is that the state, having verified the impossibility of consolidation through the application of some sort of formula, could pour money into the small school to provide the teachers and facilities it otherwise could not afford. The second is that the state could provide funds to enable students to board at schools of sufficient size from Monday through Thursday. The third solution involves the use of such devices as correspondence courses, television, and cooperative teaching assignments between schools. With this last arrangement, either a student travels to another school for a specific course not offered in his school, or the teachers of special subjects travel from school to school.

In any case, however, I am convinced that school consolidation, where at all possible, is by far the best arrangement. The solutions just mentioned should not be used as arguments to prevent consolidation but as possibilities where the state has fully determined that geography prohibits consolidation.

(See Appendix G of my Report for a breakdown of the small high school problem state by state.)

6. In order to achieve school consolidation, there must be effective state leadership. In New York, for example, the chief state school officer has the power to initiate specific reorganization proposals. The people in the proposed district make the ultimate decisions but vote on a district-wide basis throughout the proposed district. Obviously, if any one of the old districts can block the consolidation not much will be accomplished, and the chances are good that a wealthy district will react negatively to consolidation. Financial inducement at the state level in the form of aid for school construction or transportation is another factor in forwarding consolidation. Some twenty-two states have used compulsion to force very small districts to combine, and some authorities feel that the state should use its prerogative in this matter, that consolidation will be effected in no other way. Compulsory measures have been used in the form of state law alone or through joint action of state and county authorities without recourse to popular vote at all. In any event, action mandated at the state level or inspired by state leadership is needed to improve the existing situation.

7. During my visits to comprehensive high schools throughout the country I became interested in a comment I heard more than once from high school students. I asked them why they did not study more than two years of a foreign language so that they could really learn something. Their reply often was that according to a college catalogue only two years were required. To the small extent that students continue their language work in college, the requirement does no harm. But I suggest that very few students do continue the same language in college, further that many students have a bad two-year break in the eleventh and twelfth grades between study in school and college.

In general, a two-year admission requirement to college has disastrous effects, and I list it as one of the most significant factors that have produced the present distressing situation in foreign languages. A two-year requirement is worse than none because it wastes the student's time. If there is to be a requirement, it should mean mastery, or the equivalent of four years of study. It is not enough for the colleges to say that the guidance counselors and teachers should insist that bright students exceed the two-year requirement while in high school. In the final analysis, the attitude toward language study in American high schools can be no stronger than that in American colleges and universities. As long as language study is slighted in college, it will continue to be slighted in high school. The national interest demands a change in attitude.

8. An interesting example of the way people whose mother tongues differ tend to think in different terms was brought to my attention in a Swiss canton not long ago. Two separate systems of schools were operated in the chief city of the canton, one for the children of the German-speaking inhabitants, the other for the French-speaking. This division was carried on in the pre-university school, in which, however, the French-speaking pupils were learning German and the German-speaking pupils French. Several years before the completion of the course, the mastery of the two languages by all the pupils was sufficient to allow instructions to be carried on in either language. Yet the separation was continued until the end of the school course, because, as one of the officials said, "German-speaking people *think* so differently from French-speaking people that it would be impossible to instruct them together in one class!" What was obvious to a Swiss is almost incomprehensible to one who has never carried the study of any foreign language far enough to approach a mastery of it.

9. In more than one instance that I can think of, a young American has been assigned to the staff of the U.S. High Commissioner's office in Bonn or Berlin who knew no German but had acquired a mastery of French. In each case, with the aid of a tutor, the person in question before very long was rapidly acquiring a working knowledge of German. He progressed rapidly because he knew how to tackle the job of learning a foreign language and had confidence in his ability to succeed in the task. In marked contrast stands my memory of other individuals who came without having studied any foreign language long enough to acquire anything approaching a mastery, either from the point of view of speaking or reading. Such people, as a rule, struggle almost hopelessly with a tutor in their endeavors to acquire by part-time study enough knowledge of German to be of some service to them.

My thesis that mastery of one language means that a second or third can be learned much more quickly is based on more than my own experience. During the past two years I have talked with countless numbers of foreign language teachers, who agree wholeheartedly with me. I realize full well that this line of argument soon enters the thorny problem of transfer of training, but I have yet to see any research that invalidates my claim that mastery of one language cuts down on the time involved in learning a second. By mastery I do not mean a two-year exposure which, I agree, probably does little to aid in the acquisition of a second language.

10. See my Report, p. 91 and p. 123. I should like to emphasize particularly the significance of vocational courses in the eleventh and twelfth grades, occupying about half the student's time, from the point of view of influencing the attitude of many students toward the entire school program. Judging from my experience, those students in vocational elective programs had an attitude of seriousness toward their work, a degree of commitment to their studies, which was very commendable. It often seemed greater than that of the boy of medium ability who was forced by an ambitious parent to take an academic program in which he was learning little, perhaps failing. These students in vocational programs knew why they were in high school; they saw a purpose to their labor, and this attitude seemed to carry over into their required English and social studies courses as well. On page 31 of my Report are what I call career commitment diagrams; they reveal the degree of purposeful direction among the students in a few of the schools I visited. I cannot agree with those who would put off such tentative career decisions until after high school. I think it unrealistic to expect motivation among students whose studies have no apparent goal.

11. Recommendation 21 of my Report calls for a required course in the senior year on American problems or American government. This recommendation is based on classes I saw in operation in various schools. Contrary to other required subjects in which students are grouped according to ability, this course is grouped heterogeneously so that students with different vocational goals, abilities, and interests can freely discuss critical issues in American life. This course in the twelfth grade presupposes a thorough course in American history earlier in high school. Here the future corporation executive and the future labor leader first sit down and share viewpoints about a variety of questions. That such a course exists in schools within a free society and does not exist in a totalitarian state is a significant fact that needs no further underlining. This

course, together with other general education courses and student activities such as clubs, athletics, and student councils, as well as effectively organized homerooms, is one of the means employed to promote qualities of good citizenship.

See Recommendation 20 of my Report for a discussion of the importance of homerooms in promoting social cohesion and student morale. That school administrators are well aware of the social function of our schools is clear when one picks up a high school student's handbook. In addition to a listing of the courses available, one finds a wide variety of clubs and activities that are designed to appeal to all kinds of student interests. While the homeroom is a cross section of the student body in terms of academic ability and interest, these clubs, which include everything from auto mechanics, to dramatics, to singing groups, have as one of their purposes the promotion of friendly cooperation between students with perhaps widely divergent vocational goals yet similar avocational interests. Athletics, of course, can do much to further morale and spirit within the school as well as enthusiasm for the school within the community. There is the danger, naturally, that all these activities can be carried too far. I have seen schools where I thought emphasis might better be placed on the phase of the curriculum that dealt with the students' studies.

12. For example, there are two major education bills before congressional committees as I write (June 1959). The Murray-Metcalf Bill proposes flat grants to the states based on each state's estimated school-age population. The Eisenhower Administration proposal is designed to stimulate classroom construction by offering federal aid toward the retirement of bond issues. These and other proposals involving tax rebates, federally financed scholarships, etc., certainly do not stress the important fact that there are some states whose financial status is far worse than others.

A few words about the history of federal aid to education may be in order at this point. As Butts and Cremin make plain in *A History of Education in American Culture*, the first large-scale proposal for federal participation in education came shortly after the end of the Civil War. Since then, proposals for massive federal aid to education have been made at least every decade (Butts and Cremin, p. 370–375, 534–538, 580–584). The National Advisory Committee on Education appointed by President Hoover was clearly established in order to throw light on this highly controversial issue. President Hoover in his annual message to Congress on December 3, 1929, said: "In view of the considerable difference of opinion as to policies which should be pursued by the Federal Government with respect to education, I have appointed a committee representative of the important educational associations and others to investigate and present recommendations." (The Committee included the director of the American Council on Education, C. R. Mann, who was chairman; J. W. Crabtree, the secretary of the National Education Association; and a number of professors of education, public school administrators, university presidents, and prominent citizens. Henry Suzzallo, president of the Carnegie Foundation, was Director of Studies.)

The recommendations of the Committee regarding matching grants and federal grants in aid of specialized education have already been referred to (see note 23 to Chapter I); the developments since the report was rendered in 1931 have been in a direction opposite to that recommended by the Committee. As for aid to education generally, the Committee recommended "further and continuing studies of tax systems, distribution of national income," etc., to answer two questions:

"First: How far should the Federal Government properly grant funds either to the States in support of specially designated institutions or directly to particular institutions?

"Secondly: What are the right uses of the remainder of the public domain in the States for the uses of education?"

The Committee then proceeded to recommend that "all future grants to States [should be] grants in aid of education in general, expendable by each State for any or all educational purposes as the State itself may direct."

Because of the change in administration which took place shortly after the report was made public, and the deepening of the Depression, the attention of the federal government was directed not to the areas indicated by the Committee but to educational implications of nationwide unemployment. What happened in the depression years has been described in a pamphlet issued jointly by the Educational Policies Commission of the NEA and the American Council on Education in 1945.

"Following 1929 a mounting number of school systems, and especially those in the poorer sections of the Nation, found themselves in an increasingly serious financial situation. . . . By 1933, it was clear that something had to be done or many children would be denied all educational opportunity.

"The Federal Government responded through a series of indirect measures. Relief funds were made available by the WPA to help keep schools open. . . . Under the Public Works Administration,

178

large sums were also made available for new buildings. . . . These PWA funds were distributed directly to local school systems by a non-educational agency in Washington. The federal Office of Education had no official relationship to this process. The state departments of education were also often ignored. . . .

"The National Youth Administration was the farthest advance of the Federal Government into the field of educational control during the Depression. This agency was established to meet the serious youth problem which arose in the middle 1930's. . . . In the NYA the National Government set up its own organization responsible for the direct administration of youth education. The NYA was established as a temporary organization to relieve unemployment among youth. The federal officers in charge soon made it clear, however, that it was to be a permanent agency. The NYA began to establish schools of its own in direct competition with established public school systems. The youth who attended these schools were paid from federal funds." (See *Federal-State Relations in Education*, Washington: National Education Association and American Council on Education, March 1945.)

After reciting these facts, the authors of the joint pamphlet spoke of the "trend toward the federalizing of education" caused by the distribution of "hundreds of millions of dollars for the payment of teachers and for the erection of school buildings in communities where war industries and training centers have been established." The purpose of the pamphlet was "to warn the American people of an ominous trend toward the federalizing of education" on the one hand. On the other a vigorous plea was entered for federal grants to assure an adequate financial basis for education everywhere in the nation, the distribution to be on an objective basis which leaves the control of education to the states and localities.

I doubt if a candid review of the last fourteen years would indicate that the dangers envisaged in the document issued in 1945 have, in fact, materialized. Proponents of federal aid for the general purpose of the public schools are always ready to point out that for years the federal government has been concerned with public schools in one way or another. As Burke writes (*Financing Public Schools*, p. 383), most states admitted to the Union after adoption of the Federal Constitution were created out of territories, and in these territories Congress had made provisions for a public school system. Furthermore, for admission to statehood, Congress has stipulated requirements as to a public school system in a number of instances. From time to time in the nineteenth century, the federal government made grants of land to states in support of schools and also monetary grants. In more recent times, beginning with the Morrill Act of 1862, Congress has made land grants or appropriated money to the states for aiding education in special fields, such as mechanical and agricultural arts (the land-grant colleges) and vocational education (note 23 to Chapter I). The educational provisions of the G.I. Bill of Rights, of course, are another example of Congress' providing money for education.

13. Those who are unfamiliar with the methods of reporting school expenditures should be warned at the outset of certain pitfalls. It is customary to distinguish between *total* annual expenditures and *current* annual expenditures. The first figure includes capital outlays and interest on indebtedness; the second, operating expenditures of which professional salaries represent something like seventy percent. For example, the February 1959 *Research Bulletin* of the NEA (vol. 37, no. 1, p. 5) gives the estimated total expenditures for the school year 1958–59 as 14.3 billion dollars and the estimated current expenditures as 10.7 billion. For the same year, Otto Eckstein gives the figure of 13.8 for total costs, *excluding interest* (*Trends in Public Expenditures in the Next Decade*, New York: Committee for Economic Development, April 1959, p. 45). When one attempts to reduce national, state, or local expenditures to a per pupil basis, another complication arises. The calculation may be made either on the basis of the total number of pupils enrolled or on the basis of the average daily attendance (ADA). Using the figures given in the NEA *Bulletin*, one finds the 1958–59 current expenditure per pupil enrolled is estimated at $310 (10.7 billion dollars divided by 34.6 million — the number of pupils enrolled in the public schools). However, the ADA current expenditure per pupil is given in the same bulletin as $340. In other words, the ADA figure is something like ten percent higher. Most costs given at the state and local level are on an ADA basis. The ADA current expenditures per pupil varied in 1958–59 among the states from $164 in Alabama to $535 in New York.

It will be noted that for the nation as a whole the current expenditures are about seventy-five percent of the total. The 1958–59 estimated total expenditure per pupil enrolled is $415 (14.3 billion dollars divided by 34.6 million pupils) as compared with the $310 current expenditure. Whether this same percentage figure holds for a state or a local district will depend, of course, on the capital expenditure during the year and the way the amortization of the cost of the capital construction is handled. This can be determined in each instance from the figures published. In general, it is safe to say that the taxpayers' burden for public education is not determined by the costs of construction of the school buildings as much as is often supposed. This fact is important in connection with many criticisms of the public schools that come from the indignant taxpayer who sees large, modern schools being erected in his community. No one can deny that in some instances school houses have been built that were unnecessarily expensive, and the citizens concerned with the local schools (Chapter III) should be on the lookout for such extravagance. But even an increase in capital expense of the entire school plant of twenty-five percent would mean an increase in total annual costs per pupil of only about six percent (assuming the current expenditure is 75 percent of the total).

14. See my Report, p. 50. The case of the English teachers is a striking example of the relation between the size of the staff and the type of instruction that can be offered. If an English teacher is responsible for as many as 180 pupils (as is the case in a number of schools I have visited), he or she cannot find the time to correct a weekly theme. As a consequence, few themes are written. Trials are being made in a number of high schools with "lay readers" to assist the English teachers in correcting the themes. It is too early to be sure of the complete success of this scheme and the possibility of thus employing laymen on a part-time basis to help overloaded teachers. But even the employment of lay readers adds considerably to the cost per pupil.

15. See *An Essay on Quality in Public Education* by the Educational Policies Commission (Washington: National Education Association, 1959). Two paragraphs are worth quoting (p. 16–17):
"In any school system there should be enough competent professionals to ensure that every pupil receives needed attention. Where this standard is met, classes are of various sizes, depending on subjects taught and the characteristics of the student body. If the school program is to provide wide opportunities, and if the supplementary services of guidance counselors, librarians, coordinators, and administrators are to be available, there is obviously some minimum staff below which needed professional services cannot be supplied. Experience in good school systems indicates that this minimum is about fifty professionals per thousand pupils. These professionals might be distributed in many ways. In some cases as many as forty might be classroom teachers. If somewhat larger classes are feasible, thereby decreasing the number of teachers, the individual assistance each pupil needs for maximum achievement can be provided only if the number of supplementary professional personnel rises to compen-

sate. If fewer than fifty professionals are available per thousand pupils, some of the elements of a program of high quality are likely to be slighted.

"It should be emphasized that this ratio is a minimum. Better services to pupils, and consequently higher quality education, can be provided with a competent staff of larger size. In communities where schools are best supported, staffs range up to seventy professionals per thousand pupils."

One should note that the argument for fifty professionals per one thousand pupils does not rest upon an assumption of small classes. Staff size, especially the presence of a variety of professional personnel, may be more important than class size.

16. National Education Association *Research Bulletin* cited, p. 6 and p. 11. See also the NEA Research Division's *Rankings of the States*, Research Report 1959-R4, for facts about such matters as teachers' salaries and expenditures per pupil. In all fairness, one must note that revenues for school purposes have increased greatly during the past ten years — in fact, at an average yearly rate of 9.4 percent for a total gain of 145.2 percent. During this time, the relative shares of local, state, and federal school revenues have remained fairly stable. Despite the formidable revenue increase, the question remains whether this rate of growth is indeed sufficient for either the present or the future needs of the schools. (See the following note.)

17. See *National Policy and the Financing of the Public Schools* (Washington: Educational Policies Commission, 1959), p. 14. The Commission in its earlier document, *An Essay on Quality in Education*, arrives at the conclusion that "in a school district of adequate size the minimum annual per pupil current expenditure needed today to provide a good educational program is about twelve percent of the salary necessary to employ a qualified beginning teacher in that district." The basis of this conclusion is given in detail in the appendix of the document. The calculation starts from the following premises: (a) there should be at least fifty professionals per thousand pupils, or one per twenty (note 15, above); (b) the average of all the salaries of a professional staff should not be less than something like 1.7 times the starting salary (this assumption is supported by tables showing ideal distribution of salary levels); (c) the salaries of the professional staff make up about seventy percent of the annual current expenditures of a school system. From the first two assumptions it follows that the per pupil expenditure for professional salaries should be 1.7/20 of the starting salary, and, combining this with the third assumption, we

arrive at the figure of about 12 percent ($1.7/20 = .85$; $.85/.70 = .124$ or 12.4 percent).

The Educational Policies Commission in its most recent publication (p. 13) states: "The average salary offered by industry to 1958 college graduates was $4356 for women and over $5000 for men. . . . This suggests a national average exceeding $4500." If we take $4500 as the desired average beginning teacher's salary, we find that according to the formula just derived the per pupil expenditures in the United States should be $540 (12 percent of $4,500), and, since there are approximately 35 million pupils enrolled in the public schools, the total annual expenditure should be 18.9 billion dollars. During 1958–59 the figure was 10.7 billion. In other words, the "educational deficit," according to these calculations, is 8.2 billion dollars.

Another calculation of the "educational deficit" might be as follows. Assume that the present per pupil current expenditures in New York represent something approaching a satisfactory level for the entire nation, and that this figure is around $500. (For 1958–59, on a per pupil enrolled basis the estimated figure in $485.) Then the total current expenditures in dollars should be 500×35 million, or 17.5 billion, which as compared with the current figure of 10.7 yields a "deficit" of 6.8 billion, or about $200 per pupil enrolled in the entire country. This calculation is simpler than that of the preceding paragraph. Also, it would be more acceptable to some people as it appears to contain no assumption of what constitutes an average competitive salary for beginning teachers. However, it does assume a uniform per pupil cost, and, in view of the present wide differences between states, this assumption can be regarded as both unrealistic and unjustified. As a consequence, some will consider even the figure of 6.8 billion dollars too large.

Still further calculations are possible. Two of the Rockefeller Brothers Reports published in 1958 call for a doubling of expenditures by 1967 (*The Challenge to America: Its Economic and Social Aspects* and *The Pursuit of Excellence: Education and The Future of America*, Garden City: Doubleday, 1958). The NEA *Research Bulletin* previously cited estimates that total expenditures in 1957–58 for the public schools were 13.1 billion dollars (p. 5). Doubling this figure means expenditures of 26.2 billion in 1967–68. Eckstein (p. 45) projects school expenditures in 1968 as 19.3 billion at the local and state levels. (This projection does not include interest charges; it does include assumptions of an increasing school population, slightly increasing resources, and a two percent rise in teachers' salaries each year.) The difference between the 19.3 billion projection and the 26.2 billion need is about a seven billion dollar "deficit." The President's Science Advisory Committee issued a Report in May 1959 (*Education for the Age of Science*, Washington, Government Printing Office) that also urges the doubling of expenditures but gives no date as a goal. If we double our 1958–59 expenditures by 1968, we would spend 28.6 billion for our public schools. (The NEA Research Division estimates that total expenditures in 1958–59 were 14.3 billion.) Subtracting Eckstein's projected expenditure of 19.3 billion from the 28.6 billion we have a "deficit" of over nine billion dollars.

Clearly, all calculations of the "educational deficit" are only approximations and contain within them many hidden assumptions and variables which affect greatly any conclusions. I have indicated a few estimates of educational need; I know there are many others.

18. Eckstein (*Trends in Public Expenditures*, table 2, p. 9) gives, for 1959, cash expenditures of 38.4 billion and receipts of 37 billion dollars for the combined state and local budgets. His "medium" projection for the total state and local budgets in 1968 is 50.3 billion dollars in receipts and 53.7 billion dollars in expenditures, with a deficit of 3.4 billion dollars. And this projection assumes no major change in the cost per pupil for public education.

19. The projections for expenditures for mutual security are given by Eckstein (table 3, p. 13) as 3.8 billion dollars for 1959, and they are assumed to remain essentially constant until 1968. For the AEC, the 1959 figures is 2.6 billion dollars, and it is estimated it will rise to 3.5.

20. For a brief history of the efforts to persuade Congress to appropriate large sums annually for the general use of the public schools, see note 12 to Chapter II. As I have earlier pointed out, groups of educators during the last thirty years have repeatedly urged general aid to the states without conditions attached, but actually federal funds for specialized aspects of education have increased in this period, and the conditions of expenditures have been to a considerable degree determined in Washington. To be sure, considerable scope is left to the states in almost all cases. For example, under the Smith-Hughes Act the states were free to determine whether the vocational courses at the high school level were to be offered in separate vocational schools or in a widely comprehensive high school. In three states the decision was made to have only separate vocational schools. The history of this financing of specialized education by the federal government could be cited by those who have no worries about undue federal influence if large-scale

federal aid for public schools should be instituted. But it is one thing to appropriate annually tens of millions of dollars, and quite another to appropriate billions. Furthermore, because of the specialized nature of the education for which federal money is now appropriated, it is possible for a group of citizens deeply interested in this phase of education to be continually active on its behalf and block any moves to reduce the annual appropriation or attach new conditions thought unwise.

To my mind, if Congress decides to appropriate billions of dollars annually for the general use of the public schools, careful consideration should be given to a recommendation of the National Advisory Committee on Education appointed by President Hoover (note 12 to Chapter II). A majority of this Committee recommended the creation of the position of a Secretary of Education who should have under his jurisdiction all the federal expenditures for education, including, of course, all the activities carried on by the Office of Education. If the federal government is to go into the educational business in a big way, there must be a strong department of the executive branch of the government if conflicting pressure groups are not to determine the size of the appropriations and the conditions attached to the grants. I am aware that in all the bills thus far presented there are declarations concerning the intent of Congress to leave all educational matters in the hands of each state and the local boards. But no Congress can bind a subsequent Congress. Moreover, I doubt if it is possible to provide for an equitable and reasonable distribution of funds for the general uses of the public schools without having Congress make a number of important decisions affecting education (see note 21 below).

21. A flat grant per capita (or per child enrolled in the public schools) to each state to be used by the state as it sees fit for public education is an attractive formula for those who are worried about federal interference with the schools. If the practice could be established that each state was to receive so much per child per year, the need for either federal executive review of the national situation each year or congressional restriction on the use of the money would be minimized.

While there are advantages in the per capita grant idea from the point of view of minimizing the possibility of federal interference, there are grave difficulties in justifying such a proposal. In the first place, it largely ignores the truly desperate straits of the very poor states. In the second place, the richer states will be under great temptation to replace state and local funds now used for education by federal money, unless there is a congressional requirement that would prevent such a practice. And if Congress requires that the state and local expenditures for public schools be continued at present or higher levels, some states are going to receive more money than they need. In New York, for example, the present average expenditure per pupil is not far from the contemplated standard for the entire nation. Is New York to be required to spend $200 more per pupil than it already does if a flat grant of this amount is provided in the bill? The same question could be asked about what would happen in some of the other wealthy states which now have high average expenditures per pupil.

Considerations of this sort lead one to the conclusion that what is required is not a flat grant of federal money, but a federal foundation or equalization program (p. 28–29). For example, Congress might fix as a goal for average expenditure per pupil enrolled throughout the nation the figure of $500 (essentially the New York figure — see note 17). Then each state would receive only as much federal money as would be required to come up to this figure *without reducing the present state and local support*. This would mean that New York and certain other states would receive little or no federal money for school support while other states would receive an amount which, when taken with the present support, would bring the average state figure to $500. It seems clear that in developing any such equalization formula a strong federal executive agency would have to collect a vast amount of information and be ready to support the recommended formula before Congress every year. Difficult decisions would have to be made first by the Administration and then by Congress. A new chapter in American public education would, indeed, have opened.

22. The authors of *The Pursuit of Excellence* (p. 35) write as follows:

"It is this weakness in the state and local taxing systems more than anything else that gives rise to current proposals for increased federal support of education. For those who wish to resist or postpone the resort to federal funds and at the same time not constrict educational services there seems to be only one alternative: a thorough, painful, politically courageous overhaul of state and local tax systems."

See, also, articles on tax reform in *Fortune* (March, May, and June of 1959). The article in the June issue makes specific recommendations for tax reform at the state and local levels.

III. THE CITIZEN'S RESPONSIBILITY

1. See note 3 to Chapter II.

2. *Education in the U.S.S.R.* (Washington: Government Printing Office, 1957). This report, which deals largely with the ten-year schools, must now be read with Khrushchev's memorandum and the changes under way in Soviet education in mind (see note 4 to Chapter I).

3. "Truce Among Educators," *Teachers College Record*, vol. XLVI, December 1944, p. 157–63 and also *Educational Digest*, vol. X, April 1955, p.21–27. The animosity generated in many universities in this century between the professors of education and the professors of the liberal arts has had most serious consequences for the development of our public schools. The blame for this unfortunate situation cannot with justice be assigned solely to one camp. Part of the difficulty arose from the failure of the professors in the liberal arts colleges to follow with sufficient interest and understanding the transformation of the public high schools in this century (see Chapter IV). Part of the difficulty, however, came from the intemperate attacks of some professors of education on the classical academic curriculum, as well as from the fact that many developed a terminology of their own (as did some social scientists in the other faculties also); insistence on talking about "number skills" and the "language arts," not to mention "life adjustment," was annoying to the majority of the members of the faculties of a liberal arts college or university. Furthermore, during the 1920's, the professors of education and their former students, now public school administrators and teachers, more or less had things their own way with local school boards and state boards of education. As I suggest in Chapter IV, it was only after World War II that the American public awoke to what had happened to their schools. It is not overstating the case to say that because of the split within the academic world the educational profession does not today enjoy the full confidence of the American public; influential sections of public opinion are critical if not hostile. In these circumstances, the local school board and its agent, the superintendent, cannot rely exclusively on professional opinion and are bound to have far more to say about educational matters than would otherwise be the case.

To underline the point I am attempting to make in this note, let me remind the reader of the European situation. The idea of state-supported schools for training teachers was brought to the United States from Europe (particularly Prussia) more than a century ago (see p. 161). The merging of such teacher-training colleges into the universities of the United States was a slow process and did not even start until towards the end of the nineteenth century. No one can deny that the attempt to date has been, with few exceptions, something less than a complete success. In Germany the staff of the *pre-university schools* is trained in the universities, not in the separate pedagogical institutes in which elementary teachers are trained. The resulting sharp cleavage between teachers in the elementary schools and the pre-university schools has had its unfortunate consequences, but the university professors and the teachers in the pre-university schools have remained in close contact. For a discussion of the problems connected with the training of teachers in Germany, see Wenke, *Education in Germany* (p. 77–85) and Chapter V of Lindergun's *Germany Revisited*.

There has been no loss of confidence in the schools on the part of the university people in Germany such as has characterized the United States in the last twenty-five years. As indicated in what follows, I am optimistic that this confidence will be restored through the cooperation of professors of education, professors of the liberal arts, and high school teachers and administrators. When this process, which is only now beginning, has been completed, professional views and traditions will play a larger part than they do at present in determining policy in many school systems.

4. To be sure, one cannot deny that old antagonisms die hard. Nonetheless, I have heard of rumors of agreement between faculties of education and faculties of arts and sciences, where formerly there has been either open hostility or icy silence. In June 1958, there took place the Second Bowling Green Conference on "The Education of Teachers: New Perspectives." Involved were eight sponsoring organizations, all of them influential professional groups, and some fifty cooperating organizations, all segments of the profession — in higher education, in elementary and secondary education, in the state administrative organizations — united in a common cause for constructive action to improve the preparation of teachers in the United States. Several examples of cooperative "all-institution" approaches to the education of teachers in universities were given. For the official report of the conference, see *The Education of Teachers: New Perspectives* (Washington: National Education Association, 1958). A similar conference was held in June 1959.

5. "On the Conflict Between the 'Liberal Arts' and the 'Schools of

Education'." a report prepared by the Committee on the Teaching Profession of the American Academy of Arts and Sciences: Howard M. Jones, chairman; Francis Keppel; and Robert Ulich. The report appeared in *The ACLS Newsletter*, vol. V. no. 2 (1954), and has been reprinted separately by the American Council of Learned Societies, 34 East 46th Street, New York 17, New York.

6. The Supreme Court decisions in regard to racial segregation in the schools and the reaction to these decisions illustrate the complexities of the framework within which educators must operate in the United States. On two previous occasions at least (note 9 to Chapter I), the Supreme Court has decided that the United States Constitution and its Amendments have set limits to what the people of a state may do with their public schools. In the Orgeon decision a law initiated by popular referendum was negated, and in the Nebraska case a law passed by the state legislature was declared invalid. In short, at least since the Fourteenth Amendment was adopted, the United States Constitution has provided one set of boundary conditions for our schools. As repeatedly pointed out in this volume, the state constitutions and enactments of the state legislatures set another; the reaction of parents as expressed through pressures on the local boards represents a third. Fortunately, for the most part, the different portions of the legal and sociological framework have not been incompatible. Where they are, it is clearly not a matter for professional educators to attempt to settle.

For discussions of the effects of the Supreme Court's decisions, see Harry S. Ashmore, *The Negro and the Schools* (Chapel Hill: University of North Carolina Press, 1954); Omar Carmichael and Weldon James, *The Louisville Story* (New York: Simon and Schuster, 1957); Don Shoemaker, editor, *With All Deliberate Speed* (New York: Harper, 1957).

7. See note 10 to Chapter II.

8. For statistical purposes, the scholastic aptitude of all the children in a grade has considerable significance. This can be determined by fairly reliable tests. Expressed in terms of the I.Q. of the entire ninth grade population of the country, the distribution curve is estimated to be of a bell shape with a median of around 100.

I have visited many high schools where the median I.Q. of the ninth grade was only a little higher than this figure. (The median for the upper grades is apt to be higher because of the drop-out of the less able students.) In some communities, however, the median I.Q. of the ninth grade may be as high as 115 or 120. This corresponds to a

NORMAL DISTRIBUTION OF SCHOLASTIC APTITUDE

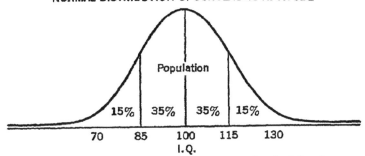

(Based on California test of mental maturity-short form)

shift in the bell shaped distribution curve to the right and means that, instead of fifteen percent of the grade having the potentialities of the academically talented, as many as fifty percent of the grade may be in this category. The reasons for the great differences in the distribution of scholastic aptitude of children in different communities is worthy of more study. A similar and somewhat parallel difference is found in regard to the reading abilities of the children in a particular grade. In some schools as many as fifteen to twenty percent of the ninth grade are reading only at the fifth or sixth grade level; in other schools only a small percentage will be thus retarded. I am not prepared to express an opinion as to the extent to which the differences to which I have referred reflect different cultural levels of the homes, different social situations, and different effectiveness of the instructors in the lower grades. Of one thing I am convinced — namely, that the very slow reader, by the time he or she reaches the ninth grade, presents a special and important problem. (See my Report, p.55).

9. As I have pointed out in my Report on the comprehensive high school (p. 60), I believe that it is impossible today to speak meaningfully of college entrance requirements. The admission requirements of our four-year colleges cover a wider range than ever before. Today some four-year liberal arts colleges have to refuse admission to many who a generation earlier would have qualified for entrance; the pressure of applicants has made it necessary for these institutions to be highly selective. Unless a candidate has the developed scholastic aptitude that places him in the upper fifteen percent of the twelfth grade population on a national basis, his chances of being

admitted to a number of well-known colleges are small indeed. At least one engineering school maintains such high standards for admission that a boy whose mathematical aptitude places him lower than the top small percentage can hardly hope to be admitted. At the other end of the scale are certain state universities which are required by law to admit all graduates of the high schools within the state. I am told that certain private institutions exist which admit a boy or girl with very little academic talent and hardly any record of achievement in mathematics, science, or a foreign language. Among the various proposals for improving the work of our high schools, the one that I am sure will *not* work is the suggestion that we raise the college entrance requirements throughout the nation.

10. See Appendix F of my Report for a description of the various vocational programs for which federal aid is available. These include trade and industrial programs, distributive education (often with what is called work experience since pupils work on regular outside jobs part time during the last two high school years), home economics, and agriculture. Approximately half the student's time in the eleventh and twelfth grades is spent in these vocational programs. Quite obviously, for these programs to be effective, they must be tied to employment possibilities within the community. For this purpose, a joint labor-management committee is often helpful in developing a program to fit the particular community's needs.

I am in favor of including vocational work in a regular comprehensive high school and not in a separate vocational school, since I think it well that the future manager of industry and the future craftsman have as close a relationship as possible in our free society. Too often separate vocational schools become dumping grounds for slow learners and discipline cases, and often these schools have an unfortunate stigma attached to them. I realize, however, that in large cities separate vocational schools are the rule, generally for economy's sake. It would be prohibitively expensive to duplicate machinery in all the schools. In New York City, for example, in 1956 there were 85 high schools, 31 of them vocational schools enrolling about twenty-five percent of all the high school students. In addition to vocational schools in the large cities, there are three states where these schools exist throughout the state — Wisconsin, Connecticut, and Massachusetts.

11. See note 2 to Chapter II on the California situation. Where local community colleges exist, it is possible for a highly gifted student (some two or three percent of the population on a national

basis) to anticipate college work in one or more subjects in his senior high school year by attending classes in the community college. Similarly, for those who have developed mechanical skills through a Smith-Hughes vocational program, it is possible to build on this training by further vocational work in the community college. For example, a tool and die worker may develop into a tool designer.

12. For the argument in favor of the study of a foreign language for four years see p. 40–43. In developing the argument. I did not specify which language was to be studied in school. To my mind the choice is of secondary importance because the main point is to know what it means to learn a language. I do have in mind, however, a modern language (French, Spanish, or German). If Latin is elected, it should be studied for not less than four years in high school, and the study should be continued in college. Only when a boy or girl is in a position to read Latin with considerable ease is he or she in a position to obtain the advantages of the type of classical education which for a few, at least, was so rewarding a generation or two ago. With the growing tendency to start instruction in a modern foreign language in the lower grades (see my Report, p. 72), the place for Latin in the high school may well be that of a second foreign language. For certain types of students the study of Latin started in grade ten and *continued in college* would be most rewarding. What is *not* rewarding is the curriculum so often found today — Latin in grades nine and ten, French in grades ten and eleven, no language studied in college or, at best, exposure to one year more of French which rarely results in any command of the language.

13. The scores on a scholastic aptitude test (of which there are several types) must be used with caution when the future plans of an individual student are concerned. In well organized schools, the guidance officer uses the scores on such tests (often given in every grade) together with the pupil's achievement in various subjects and the teachers' estimates in advising on the elective program. For statistical purposes, however, the errors in such tests do not vitiate the sort of conclusions about a school which can be drawn from a summary of the programs of, say, 100 pupils with scores which place them in the upper fifteen percent on a national basis. Perhaps as many as five or ten out of 100 may be out of place, but the potentialities of the group as measured by the test scores will not be materially affected by this fact.

See Appendix H of my Report for detailed instructions on how to make an academic inventory. I consider the inventory one of the most important bits of information one can have if a sensible and factual discussion is to take place about the education of the bright students in a particular school. There have been many schools which appear to be doing a good job — appear, for example, to match up well with most of my recommendations — but fail to take an academic inventory, which, perhaps, in light of the present world situation, is the most important recommendation of all.

I should point out that there are many professional educators who are aware of the kind of world in which we live and the necessity for developing special skills among youth with academic talent. In February 1958, the National Education Association, with the aid of the Carnegie Corporation, sponsored a Conference on the Identification and Education of the Academically Talented Student in the American Secondary School. This Conference was followed up by a Project on the Academically Talented Student, again sponsored by the NEA and aided by the Carnegie Corporation. Under director Charles E. Bish, the Project provides consultant services to state and local systems, collects research data, organizes study conferences, and is in the process of publishing a series of booklets covering content in particular subject areas.

See *Mathematics for the Academically Talented Student* and *Science for the Academically Talented Student* (Washington: National Education Association, 1959). Both are reports of conferences, sponsored by the NEA Project and the National Council of Teachers of Mathematics and the National Science Teachers Association respectively. See, also, the 1958 Conference Report, *The Identification and Education of the Academically Talented Student in the American Secondary School* (Washington: National Education Association, 1958).

14. Appendix D of my Report shows the results of twenty-two academic inventories in widely comprehensive high schools. The figures reveal a wide diversity in the programs taken by the academically talented students. In one school eighty-five percent of the boys who tested in the top fifteen percent on a national basis took a total of eighteen subjects with homework in four years; seventy percent of them took nineteen subjects. Needless to say, such a wide program means that these students did not specialize in one subject to the neglect of another; they took four years of mathematics and three years of science, but they also took four years of English, four years of social studies, and over half of them took four years of foreign language. As a result, these boys are prepared to move in any direction they choose when they get to college; all doors are open.

On the other hand, in another school only forty percent of the academically talented boys took as many as fifteen subjects in four years. Not only were science, mathematics, and foreign languages neglected, but English and social studies as well. I submit that if an academic inventory reveals facts similar to these, the citizens of a community should get together with the school board and see what is wrong. If the facts are similar to those of the first school I described, then the school has at least been successful in getting the bright students into the proper elective courses and is, thereby, contributing to the national welfare.

Appendix E of my Report shows the results of a statewide inventory in Maryland. These results parallel what I found in the twenty-two schools whose inventories are summarized in Appendix D. Contrary to what we have been hearing, the bright boys, at least, seem to be taking mathematics and science but not foreign languages; the bright girls shy away from both. In Maryland, at least seventy-five percent of the bright boys in a number of schools took nineteen subjects, and not a few took twenty subjects. I believe the statewide publication of the pertinent facts about each high school, including the academic inventory, would lead in many cases to rapid improvement by stimulating local pride. Competition between communities in terms of the quality of the education provided might even come to approach, in popular interest, the present vigorous competition between local athletic teams.

15. The selective academic high school (tax-supported) has flourished in certain large cities along the Atlantic Coast. With one or two exceptions, such institutions have never been maintained for any length of time west of the Allegheny Mountains, not even in the large cities. Some of the more violent critics of the American public high school have, in recent years, advocated the establishment of a series of such schools. They have not been specific, however, about the requirements for admission, the management of the schools, or their financing. In some of the selective, tax-supported, academic schools the standards are so high that not more than the top five percent on a national basis could obtain admission. In others, those whose potentialities (as measured by scholastic aptitude tests) place them in the top fifteen or twenty percent are admitted. Obviously the differences between these schools are considerable, and one wonders sometimes which type the advocates of the selective school have in mind. Still a third type could be imagined — namely, a school to which any parent could send his child if he wanted a strictly academic course. But the only way such a school could operate

194

without lowering standards would be to drop those who did not show the required ability. Such a procedure would be similar to that employed in the European pre-university schools but would, in most communities, evoke a powerful protest from the parents.

Leaving aside the advantages of a comprehensive high school as an instrument for forwarding American democracy, it is my belief that more rapid progress toward providing adequate free education for the academically talented will be made by changes in the present 4000 high schools of sufficient size (note 4 Chapter II) than by attempts to set up a series of selective academic schools (see also my Report, p. 87-91).

16. Because the future of our public schools depends so much upon the informed interest of citizens in thousands of communities throughout the land, I addressed my Report to "interested citizens." In addition, I spent the greater part of the school year 1958-59 traveling around the country speaking to statewide audiences of citizens interested in public education. Most of these appearances were arranged by the National Citizens Council for Better Schools, an organization whose sole purpose is to stimulate constructive action by citizens in the behalf of better schools.

Members of the Council are citizens not professionally identified with education, and they do not represent any organization or groups. Among its many activities, the Council provides a clearing house of information about school problems and the methods citizens have used to solve them. A set of pamphlets designed to help the interested citizen and school board member is available. Information can be obtained by writing to the National Citizens Council for Better Schools, 9 East 40th Street, New York City.

No discussion of the role that citizens have in improving public education would be complete without reference to the National Congress of Parents and Teachers, commonly known as the PTA. The influence of the PTA has been conspicuous at the local level, particularly in the lower grades. I think it fair to say that these organizations throughout the United States typify the important role played by the parent as contrasted with the situation in Europe. National headquarters are at 700 North Rush Street, Chicago 11, Illinois. *The National Parent-Teacher* is published monthly September through June.

17. See note 7 to Chapter I.

18. An interesting and informative report on the struggle for the improvement of the Chicago School Board from 1933 to 1946 is to

be found in *Better Schools*, May 1959, vol. 5, no. 5, p. 13. The report of the "Committee on Inquiry into Charges of Waste and Extravagance in the Construction of School Buildings in New York City" (appointed by the State Commissioner of Education) makes some highly important points that have bearing on the situation in certain other cities. According to the *New York Times*, May 22, 1959, the Committee (composed of Dr. Henry T. Heald, President of the Ford Foundation, Dr. Herold C. Hunt, of the Harvard Graduate School of Education, and Max I. Rubin, a New York attorney) wrote as follows:

"We are convinced that it is essential for the efficient and economical construction of schools in New York and the improvement of the school system generally to eliminate all assumption of administrative powers by the [Board of Education], leaving it the freedom it needs to deliberate and act on matters of policy.

"To strengthen the board's role as a legislative body and to clarify its relationships with the Superintendent of Schools, we make the following recommendations:

"1. Legislation should be enacted eliminating borough representation. Each member should represent the entire school district.

"2. To assist the Mayor in securing the most qualified citizens for appointment to the board, it is recommended that he invite a number of organizations, representing among others, commerce, labor, law and medicine, together with the presidents of the universities within the city, to name representatives to constitute a panel. The panel's responsibility would be to nominate for each vacancy on the Board of Education from three to five qualified persons of unquestioned standing for selection by the Mayor. It is expected that the Mayor would wish to make his choice from the nominees, though legally not obligated so to do.

"3. The board should, as expeditiously as possible, cease participation in all administrative functions, and should transfer them to the office of the Superintendent of Schools.

"4. The board should act as a legislative and not as an administrative body and should continue to exercise its investigatory and judicial powers.

"5. The board should abolish all of its standing and continuing special committees.

"6. The board should carefully re-examine the need for the retention of the existing staff of its secretary.

"7. The board should reduce the size of the office staffs of individual members by eliminating the position of confidential secretary and of office workers other than one stenographer, in view of the recommended relinquishment by the board of administrative functions.

"8. The board should, in cooperation with the Superintendent, seek nation-wide counsel in the reorganization of the Superintendent's staff.

"9. Upon the recommendation of the Superintendent, the board should proceed promptly to the appointment of the best person available to head the Division of Housing and the Bureau of School Planning and Research in the Division of Housing and the employment of essential personnel in school programming and planning.

"10. The board should transfer all personnel administration, with the staff engaged thereon, to the office of the Superintendent.

"11. The board should grant to the Superintendent full authority to employ, assign and promote all personnel in the teaching and civil staff below the rank of assistant superintendent or equivalent, subject only to the necessary pro forma approval required by law. Positions of assistant superintendent or higher in the teaching and civil service staffs should be filled upon the recommendation of the Superintendent subject to review and approval by the board."

The National Citizens Council for Better Schools (note 16, above) has various case histories illustrating the role of citizens committees in supporting school board efforts on behalf of better schools. See, also, *How Can We Help Our School Boards*, a Citizens Council booklet which describes the policy-making function of the boards and the ways in which interested citizens can be of assistance.

IV. THE REVOLUTIONARY TRANSFORMATION OF THE AMERICAN HIGH SCHOOL

1. In 1910, the older eastern colleges occupied a far more important position relatively than they do today, both in the field of scholarship and in that of athletics. The fact that the student body of these institutions was then predominantly recruited from private schools explains why the faculties were but little concerned with the new problems of the public schools. Furthermore, one might assume in 1910 that the majority of students in the public schools of eastern cities who wished to go to college would enroll in specialized academic schools like the Boston Latin School. See Alexander Inglis, *Principles of Secondary Education* (Boston: Houghton Mifflin, 1918), p. 197, for a table showing the change in private and public high school enrollments 1889 to 1915. The public school figures jumped from sixty-eight to ninety percent.

For a penetrating analysis of the influence of such humanitarian groups as the settlement workers in the education field, see Lawrence A. Cremin, "The Progressive Movement in American Education: A Perspective," *Harvard Education Review*, Vol. XXVII. No. 4, Fall, 1957. He writes: "In reality, school reform and municipal reform were frequently if not always facets of the same progressive movement; to understand them as such is to expand significantly our comprehension of progressivism both in politics and in education." See also Chapter VII, "Progressive Education and Progressive Law," in M. G. White's *Social Thought in America* (Viking Press, 1949).

Another factor which helps to explain the educational transformation of 1905–1930 is the great increase in non-English-speaking immigration during the last quarter of the nineteenth century and continuing into the first quarter of the present century. Whereas less than sixty percent of the foreign-born population of the United States was non-English-speaking in 1890, twenty years later almost three quarters of this group were so classified. The secondary school faced many important problems arising out of this immigration, "involving a longer period of education and an education which should aim definitely toward the integration of large groups of different forms of social heredity." (Inglis, p. 98)

2. Inglis, p. 577. On p. 146, he writes: "During the last decade of the nineteenth century and the beginning of the present century there has been a marked increase in the attendance in the public secondary school of pupils who were not destined for higher education." On p. 370, he writes: "As long as pupils receiving the benefits of secondary education were drawn from classes whose vocations were almost entirely the higher professions, involving vocational education in higher institutions, the directly vocational aim in the secondary school was subordinated to other aims except in so far as preparation for higher institutions might be conceived as involving indirect contribution to a vocational aim. With the extension of the benefits of secondary education to the non-professional classes greater importance has necessarily been attached to the economic-vocational aim."

On p. 119, Inglis writes: "The great increase in the number of secondary school pupils is in part the result and in part the cause of the extension of the curricula to meet the diversified needs of different groups of pupils. . . . Pupils of types not attending the secondary school before 1890 now are enrolled in large numbers."

In 1913, the National Education Association appointed a Commission on the Reorganization of Secondary Education. This Commission issued thirteen separate reports, the most well-known of which was entitled *Cardinal Principles of Secondary Education* (Bulletin 1918, No. 35, Department of the Interior, Bureau of Education, Government Printing Office). On p. 8 the authors state: "In the past 25 years there have been marked changes in the secondary school population of the United States. The number of pupils has increased, according to Federal returns, from one for every 210 of the total population in 1889–90, to one for every 121 in 1899–1900. to one for every 89 in 1909–10, and to one for every 73 of the estimated total population in 1914–15. The character of the secondary school population has been modified by the entrance of large numbers of pupils of widely varying capacities, aptitudes, social heredity, and destinies in life."

3. Inglis, p. 77, Table XXV. Though the median age of 949 pupils entering New York City public high schools in 1906 was fourteen years, six months, twenty percent were a year or more older.

On p. 7, Table III, Inglis gives the data for six cities showing that the twelve-year-olds were distributed in considerable numbers over grades five, six, and seven and as many as twenty-three percent of the sixteen-year-olds still in school were enrolled in grades eight or lower.

On p. 276, Inglis writes, "The large number of over-age pupils found in the elementary school raises some serious questions concerning methods of promotion in the later grades of that school . . . the practice, hitherto obtaining, of retaining pupils chronologically, physiologically, and socially mature in the lower grades of the school system and making the complete accomplishment of prescribed amounts of elementary-school work the sole criterion for the admission of pupils to other forms of education is a practice harmful both to the school and to the pupils."

Inglis, pp. 123–127, discusses retardation and acceleration and at the end of the discussion concludes: "It would appear that the public secondary school is ill-adapted both to the needs of the duller pupil and the needs of the brighter pupil."

On p. 294 and 696, Inglis writes of "promotion of pupils by subjects rather than by grades."

The NEA Commission (*op. cit.*), p. 19. "Admission to high school is now, as a rule, based upon the completion of a prescribed amount of academic work. As a result many over-age pupils either leave school altogether or are retained in the elementary school when they are no longer deriving much benefit from its instruction. . . . *Consequently we recommend that secondary schools admit, and provide suitable instruction for, all pupils who are in any respect so mature that they would derive more benefit from the secondary school than from the elementary school."* (Italics in the original.)

4. Lawrence A. Cremin's "The Revolution in American Secondary Education, 1893–1910," *Teachers College Record*, March 1955, is an excellent account of the progressive movement and its effect on the high school curriculum.

5. Inglis, pp. 293–295, devotes four paragraphs to the purposes of the junior high school which was at that time a very new invention. Included are the arguments given by the NEA Commission (*op. cit.*, p. 17–19) which emphasized the need in grades seven, eight, and nine for a "pupil to explore his own aptitudes and to make at least provisional choice of the kinds of work to which he will devote himself." The Commission goes on to say (p. 19): "In the junior high school there should be the gradual introduction of departmental instruction, some choice of subjects under guidance, promotion by subjects, pre-vocational courses, and a social organization that calls forth initiative and develops the sense of personal responsibility for the welfare of the group."

The basic need for the junior high school as presented by Inglis seems to be tied to the fact to which he repeatedly returns — namely, the large number of youth who never reach even grade nine. Thus, he writes (p. 295): "If all pupils were destined to continue in school throughout the full twelve-year course and if the exigencies of administration made it possible, it would be advisable to have one undivided system consisting of grades one to twelve. Neither of those assumptions hold, however, and it is probable that they never can hold." And on p. 694–695, again Inglis states: "It is important that some of the phases of secondary education be operative before the majority of pupils leave school."

The curriculum of the junior high school suggested by Inglis (p. 685–687) is most interesting, required subjects (constants) occupying a decreasing amount of time as one passes from grade seven to nine. Variables (electives) include foreign languages beginning in grade seven. The choice between algebra and commercial arithmetic is to be made in grade eight.

6. Continuation school enrollment reached its peak throughout the nation in 1928 at 340,000. See L. S. Hawkins et al., p. 359 (cited in note 23 to Chapter I). The statistics here quoted and much valuable information about the continuation school in New York State were kindly supplied by Dr. Joseph R. Strobel, Assistant Commissioner for Instructional Services of the New York State Education Depart-

ment. Also, Franklin J. Keller's *Day Schools for Young Workers* (New York and London: The Century Company, 1924) and *The Changing Pattern of Continuation School Education In New York City; An Appraisal and a Prognosis*, a report prepared by a sub-committee of the Vocational High School Planning Committee, December 1956, were consulted.

7. That the Depression was responsible for the rapid falling off in the registration in the part-time continuation schools in New York State is made evident by the following statistics concerning enrollment:

1927	158,603	1932	141,626
1928	168,377	1933	104,987
1929	164,905	1934	74,949
1930	161,201	1935	54,232
1931	149,856	1936	56,250

In 1935, the legislature made attendance at school *full time* compulsory until sixteen, and no full-time employment certificates could be issued to those under sixteen, effective September 1, 1936. The sixteen-year-olds who had not graduated from high school were required to attend continuation school. Enrollments in part-time continuation schools and classes fell steadily to a low of 15,497 in 1942. In 1940, the law was again amended requiring continuation schools only in cities of over 400,000 population and districts having 1,000 minors aged sixteen who were obliged to attend such schools. In 1958, only three cities in New York State offered continuation courses: Buffalo, New York City, and Troy, the last on a voluntary basis. The enrollments were: New York City 18,787, Buffalo 500, Troy 151. It is correct to say that the continuation school has essentially disappeared.

8. Professor Inglis' chapter on "Practical and Vocational Arts" is interesting in view of what has happened since. Among the factors affecting the need for vocational instruction in the high schools, he mentions the following (p. 595): "The constantly increasing division of labor has tended to prevent those engaging in industrial activities from securing in industry itself broad training in the trades and crafts. . . . The apprentice system which formerly afforded valuable industrial education has tended to disappear, only 118,964 apprentices being accounted for in the entire country in the reports of the 1910 census. . . . The increased mobility of labor had tended to discourage attempts on the part of employers to train a body of broadly expert workmen and workwomen who may leave his

employ at any moment after he has gone to the expense of their industrial education."

9. The difference between such an arrangement and the work experience program to be found in many schools is worth consideration. Under the work experience programs, a teacher or director is responsible for both the work in school and some supervision for the work done on the job. Only students with at least average academic ability are encouraged (or usually allowed) to enroll. The number of places is highly limited because only a relatively few suitable openings are available in the community; employment opportunities not tied into an educational program are usually far greater. More high schools might well examine, it seems to me, the possibility of finding part-time jobs for certain types of students sixteen years of age or over, even if the employment is in no way related to the program of studies in the school.

The Industrial Cooperative Training Programs in New York State are examples of work experience. Young people sixteen and over who can benefit from vocational instruction are placed in jobs which involve a year or more of half-time employment. They learn skills on the job as outlined by the program coordinator and the employer, and they are paid for their work. The other half of their time is spent in school, where they take the courses regularly prescribed for high school graduation and also receive instruction in subjects related to their employment. Since 1950, there have been seventy different employment fields in which training has been provided. Note that the vocational facilities, often expensive, are not needed in the high school and, therefore, this wide variety is made possible. State aid is available for these programs. In 1957–58, 1458 students were enrolled in forty-five schools.

For descriptions of various kinds of work experience programs and an extensive bibliography on the subject, see *Work Experience Education Programs in American Secondary Schools* (Washington: U.S. Department of Health, Education and Welfare, Office of Education, Bulletin 1957, No. 5).

Index

203